GET GRANT READY SERIES
Volume I

Simple Grant Funding Research
Locating Public and Private Grant Funding Resources

NIKKI D. KIRK

Designs / www.fiverr.com/pikudesigns
Book design by Nikki Kirk
Editing by Kayli Tomasheki
Author photograph by Grant Central USA

No part of this book may be reproduced in any form or by any electronic or mechanical means including information storage and retrieval systems, without permission in writing from the author. The only exception is by a reviewer, who may quote short excerpts in a review.

I have tried to recreate events, locales and conversations from my memories of them. In order to maintain their anonymity in some instances I have changed the names of individuals and places, I may have changed some identifying characteristics and details such as physical properties, and occupations and places of residence.

Although the author has made every effort to ensure that the information in this book was correct at press time, the author and publisher do not assume and hereby disclaim any liability to any party for any loss, damage, or disruption caused by errors or omissions, whether such errors or omissions result from negligence, accident, or any other cause.

Nikki Kirk

Visit my websites at www.simplegrantresearch.info
www.kirksconsultingservices.com
www.getgrantready.com

ISBN-13: 978-1512387070

Text Copyright © 2016 by Nikki Kirk
Published by Kindle Direct Publishing,
All rights reserved.

First Printing: July 17th, 2016

DEDICATION

This book is dedicated to all of the children placed temporarily and permanently in foster care, those that ran away from homes where abuse continued after placement, and children that were never adopted and aged out of foster care. I know your plight. I have fought your hard fights. You are never far from my mind or my heart. You can do anything—be anything. If you can believe it, then you can achieve it

CONTENTS

	ACKNOWLEDGMENTS	I
1.	UNDERSTANDING THE PURPOSES OF GRANT FUNDING	1
2.	HOW TO FIND GRANT FUNDING	8
3.	COMMUNITY AND TARGET POPULATION RESEARCH	24
4.	LINKING DATA AND NEEDS TO GRANT FUNDING SOURCES	32
5.	PROGRAM PLANNING AND BUDGET DEVELOPMENT	40
6.	FINDING AND INTERPRETING PRIVATE FOUNDATION— 990 TAX RETURNS	44
7.	GRANT FUNDER AND GRANT-WRITING TERMS	48
8.	MAINTAINING YOUR DISCOVERED TREASURES	61
9.	RESEARCH ASSISTANCE: DEVELOPING RESEARCH TEAMS	64
10.	CLOSING	69

ACKNOWLEDGMENTS

I would like to express my sincerest gratitude to the many people that have supported me through this transformational journey over the past few years. I wish to extend a special thanks[1] to Dr. Cheryl Clansy and Dr. Shirley Seaborn for being sounding boards and nonprofit professional sector experts for the past four years. I must also thank all of my previous employers for providing me with the experiences and opportunities necessary to move forward and pursue my dreams. I would like to give a sincere thank you to my friend Dawn. You are an amazing woman, wonderful confidant, dream-builder, and caring friend. I'm so thankful our paths crossed.

I am also indebted to my friend Gloria Bryson for being supportive, helping me with my children, and providing me with laughter and love over the past 22+ years. You are a great motivator. I am also grateful for my friend Kori London and our love-hate relationship. We argue, fuss, disagree, get on one accord, and start the cycle all over again. Solving the world's problems with a friend like you is, though stressful, absolutely hilarious. Thanks for all of your positivity, prayers, and time for bouncing ideas.

I would like to send a big "thank you" to my editor Kayli. You are so awesome. Who knew that editing could be so depressing? I survive the processes thanks to you. I'm eternally grateful. A big thanks is also in order to Shalom for introducing me to Kayli.

Finally, I would like to thank Donna, my best friend through thick and thin for the past 15+ years, and my husband Jerry, for all of his support during this journey. You have been my proofreader, financial backer, and sounding board for a long time.

---

[1] Names have been modified or changed to protect those named.

1. UNDERSTANDING THE PURPOSES OF GRANT FUNDING

If you have purchased this book, you are likely hoping to learn how to find and eventually secure grant funding for the benefit of your organization, group, mission, target group, target area, and so forth. I would like to take the time to debunk some myths that have been floating around for some years. Sadly, you will not be able to receive assistance if you have purchased this book believing that you can find and secure grants to do the following:

- repair a home,
- buy a car or home, or
- start or expand a business.

Unfortunately, there are no grants available for such things, except through agencies that assist the poor, economically disadvantaged, senior citizens, etc. Over the years, a multitude of scams and books have taken millions of people for a ride, selling them pipe dreams of getting free government money for all kinds of nonsense. This commercial dream was a simple shenanigan—foolery, so to speak. Please allow me to clarify for you what grants are, as well as who and what types of entities are eligible to apply for grants (of any type). Primarily, organizations with an IRS[1] designated 501 (c) 3 tax-exempt status are eligible to apply for (and receive) grants from public and private grant-makers. Taken directly from the IRS' website, the explanation/definition of "exempt" purposes is as follows:

The exempt purposes set forth in section 501(c) (3) are **charitable, religious, educational, scientific, literary, testing for public safety, fostering national or international amateur sports competition, and preventing cruelty to children or animals.** *The term* **charitable** *is used in its generally accepted legal sense and includes relief of the poor, the distressed, or the underprivileged; advancement of religion; advancement of education or science; erecting or maintaining public buildings, monuments, or works; lessening the burdens of government; lessening neighborhood tensions; eliminating prejudice and discrimination; defending human and civil rights secured by law; and combating community deterioration and juvenile delinquency.* (www.irs.gov, 2015)[2]

Grant-makers award "grants" to organizations created and devoted to the purposes noted above. As you can see, for-profit businesses and personal businesses are *not* noted in this description. If you would like to determine the validity of the information provided, feel encouraged to conduct your own grant research and contact grant-makers to verify what types of organizations are funded. I have had so many people become downright defensive with me about "money from the government" (grants) being available for certain people (such as single women planning to go to college, people buying a house, or entrepreneurs wanting to start a new business [of any type]) because they have witnessed the promise of "free grants" or "free money" advertised on television or the internet. Therefore, I feel the need to address this topic before going any further. I am amazed by the multitude of individuals, who are not established as any type of tax-exempt or charitable entity in order to be eligible for grants, that believe they have a grant-worthy idea. The bottom line is that you need to do your own research on state and federal guidelines related to tax-exempt purposes and tax-exempt statuses. But enough about this topic—hopefully, you are here for the right reasons.

---

[1] Internal Revenue Service
[2] For more information on this topic, please visit: http://www.irs.gov/Charities-&-Non-Profits/Charitable-Organizations/Exemption-Requirements-Section-501%28c%29%283%29-Organizations

Now, let me begin by explaining the definition and purposes of grants, as well as who and what types of entities are eligible to apply for them.

What Is a Grant

A grant is a sum of money given by private foundations, trusts, or governmental entities (i.e. state and federal governments) to nonprofit organizations, state governments, cities, towns and municipalities, governmental entities (such as police and sheriff's departments), and colleges and universities. On occasion, individuals are awarded grants in order to conduct research. In some cases, a grant is an actual contract between the funder (the grant-maker) and the nonprofit or governmental entity. In other cases (primarily foundation grant proposal requests), private grant-makers award grants to organizations, entities, and states to perform services, offer help, or address issues/problems/needs in very specific focus areas.

Typically, the grant-maker has a set of goals and priorities for which the founder desires to use the organization's funds (an investment of sorts), but the founder of the private foundation is unable to address these issues by himself/herself. The private foundation (funder) solicits assistance to not only accomplish his/her goals, but also to further his/her missions. Grant-seekers are awarded grants when the formal (both solicited and unsolicited) proposals submitted by organizations to grant-makers demonstrate that these organizations, charities, and/or agencies are interested in and committed to addressing issues aligned with the specific focus areas or missions of those grant-makers.

What Grants Are Not

Now, let's discuss what grants are **NOT**. Grants are not awarded for the purposes of starting a business, buying business supplies, assisting the expansion of a private business, etc. There are no grants individuals can apply for to assist with home repair (for themselves or for their parents). There are no grants to help individuals pay for new or used cars. At times, there are grants made to certain, qualifying individuals to assist with the postsecondary education (e.g. federal student aid, fellowships, research), but they are disbursed by the United States Department of Education[3] via colleges, universities, and vocational schools.

Again, please do not believe any of the gimmicks sold on late-night television or on the internet. If you believe you have been scammed by one of these gimmicks, please contact the Federal Trade Commission to file a formal complaint. You must also change your thought process from believing these scams. I have received many calls and taught many classes where individuals attempt to tell me they are eligible for grants or they heard there are grants out there for… … … blah, blah, blah.
If you call any private grant-making foundation or publicly funded governmental entity (agencies funded via money collected from taxpayers), they will convey to you the same things. Most grant-makers have posted this information on their websites to forewarn individuals from preparing proposals and/or making requests that they are unable to fund. Before I close on the subject of what grants *are NOT*, allow me to give you one last warning. Please ***do not pay*** any person or business that indicates they can write grants for you that will result in you (as an individual) securing grants for purchasing or rehabbing houses, obtaining student financial aid, starting a business, or expanding a business. You will be wasting money, dreams, and time, because no such opportunities exist. Students seeking financial aid

---

[3]www.ed.gov/category/program/federal-pell-grant-program

assistance in the form of federal (or state) grants and loans can apply for them at no cost on the federal government's Free Application for Student Aid website[4].

The Difference between Public Grant Funds and Private Grant Funds

Now, let's move on to discussing the differences between public grant funding and private grant funding. When conducting grant research, you can search for both public and private grant funding. Public grants are tax dollars (state, federal, local) collected from individuals and businesses. They are used for the benefit of the general public. Cities, towns, municipalities, counties, parishes, states, and the federal government collect these taxes, then they create laws, ordinances, legislation, etc. to allocate these public funds for specific purposes or uses. Private grants are private assets (cash) set aside by families, businesses and corporations, individuals, and/or groups for a variety of charitable purposes (e.g. scholarships, research, education, youth and children, LGBTQ issues, animal welfare).

Grants become grants through many different processes, and they vary from state to state. The bottom line is that public funds are taxpayer dollars and, because those funds are collected from the public, the grants created using those funds must be used for consumption by the general public. You also need to be aware that the public funding process is *very* bureaucratic and super political, whether anyone will actually confess to it.

Public Grants

Publicly funded grant awards can vary in size ranging from very small, with amounts beginning as low as $2,500, to very large, with amounts reaching $50,000,000 or more, depending upon the awarding agency, the eligibility criteria, and the purpose for the award. The complete process, from the application process to the securement of the grant award, can take anywhere from a few months (after submission) to as long as one year.

Most federal grants require some type of cost sharing or match[5], although there are some that do not. Public funding focus areas change with the wind and the political climate. An initiative or issue can be created and funded at any time during a political cycle (also called federal and/or legislation); it may become available based on the passion or promises made by a politician, lobbying groups, advocates, etc. Managing these types of grant awards are very costly, as it requires lots of oversight and supervision.

Public grant funds (mainly federal, but some state) are reviewed by a process called an "Objective Review" or a "Panel Review." These reviews consist of persons not affiliated with the agency offering the solicitation for grant proposals or funding opportunity announcements (FOA). These reviews are held by 3-15 panel members from different states with different and/or similar backgrounds related to the purposes of the funding opportunity. This process can take from one to six weeks and can serve as the first or final obstacle when being awarded (or denied) a public grant award. Public grants are very easy to find (online), once you learn where to look, and the solicitations contain plenty of detailed information that allows potential applicants to clearly determine the criteria for eligibility, application formatting, etc. Public grant information is made available to the public free of charge. Public grants are often renewable (currently funded applicants may reapply) unless the funding opportunity has ceased, such as when the government fails to appropriate funding in the annual budget. The public grant fundir

---

[4] www.fafsa.ed.gov
[5] See definition in Chapter Nine.

process can be extremely competitive and the public funder usually has a large number of criteria that applicants must address in order to meet basic requirements. The bottom line is that public grants (of any kind) have a lot of "strings" attached. There are more requirements, more paperwork, more reporting, more oversight, more transparency, and more competition.

Private Grants

Private grant funding is money set aside by a private foundation (a legal charity entity) set up by an individual, a family, or a group of individuals for philanthropic purposes. Every state has private foundations set up for philanthropic purposes. Some private grant funders award grants nationally. Meaning, the foundation may be physically located in Iowa, but (according to the foundation's funding criteria and giving patterns) they fund 501 (c) 3 organizations all over the country. Other private foundations fund regionally/exclusively (e.g. Southeastern U.S., Western U.S.A, Israel and New York, large U.S. cities, out-of-U.S. areas); some fund specific states, while others fund specific nonprofits, regions, or focus areas within a state. Private foundations create their own funding priorities, which makes conducting grant funding research both interesting and frustrating.

Private grant funds are funds made available without government involvement. They can come from a variety of means including, but not limited to, private foundations, venture capitalists, family trusts, and some private organizations (e.g. VFW Veterans of Foreign Wars). Sometimes, they come from wealthy individuals or families that have an issue (or several) near and dear to their hearts. So, they allocate a portion of their wealth to address those issues. Much of the time, corporations set aside a portion of their earnings or assets for charitable works, calling it "corporate responsibility." It's their way of giving back to the community (or nation) for supporting them and making them successful. Because these funds come from individuals and private businesses, they are considered "private" monies. These funders give of their own free will for a variety of reasons (for the betterment of communities, people, societies, the environment, the arts, etc.). In addition to the source of funding, there are many more aspects in which private grant funds differ from public grant funds.

The application process for private grant funds is much simpler than that of public grant funds. Private grant funders tend to be willing to take more risks than the federal government. They have varying sizes of assets allocated to the purpose(s) for which the foundation was created. These types of funders are more likely to take chances on smaller nonprofits, offer opportunities for less-experienced organizations, and provide new/grass root grants for applicants with new innovative ideas. The application process tends to be much easier, but not always. There are hundreds of thousands of private foundations that will fund grant proposals by focus area (e.g. target population, geographical location, specific missions or issues) or on a local, state, regional, or national basis. Private funders may offer financial contributions in the form of grants or they may decide to provide other contributions such as computers, in-kind consulting services, software, and/or books. Application assistance with funders' grant application processes will vary by each private funder. Usually, the larger the funder, the less likely you are to actually receive personal assistance. Sizes of private grant funders vary as well. Some may consist of only a skeleton crew (two to three unpaid persons). Mid-size private foundations may have small staffs and/or a full-time program officer responsible for screening questions, letters of inquiry, and grant proposals that meet the foundation's focus area(s). Large private funders may have huge, paid staffs; they tend to be more bureaucratic, like the government. Unlike the government, though, they may not accept calls, emails, or unsolicited information.

The private grant funding application process also tends to be shorter (anywhere from 5-15 pages), with some funders opting to use a Common Grant Application and/or online grant application processes.

Grant awards from private funders can range from $500 to over $1,000,000 per year or per grant proposal. Many private funders allow grant-seekers to submit more than one proposal for different projects or programs. Many private funders do not offer reasons for rejecting proposals; it may be difficult to fix what was unsuitable in your grant application (if anything at all) in order to prepare for resubmission.

The nice thing about private grant funders, especially local community foundations, is that grant-seekers have an opportunity to build/develop relationships with program officers and foundation board members that may be responsible for making decisions on grant awards. Another nice thing about private grant funders is that the oversight, management, and reporting requirements are significantly less burdensome.

Additional Resources

I hope that you have learned a little bit about the differences between public and private funding. Using the online resources below, you can conduct additional research that may help you further develop your understanding of the two different types of funding.

- **Kent State University**
  http://literacy.kent.edu/Oasis/grants/publicVSprivate.html
- **Wikipedia**
  http://en.wikipedia.org/wiki/Grant_%28money%29
- **Small Business Chronicles**
  http://smallbusiness.chron.com/difference-between-public-vs-private-grant funding-12449.html
- **Investopedia**
  http://www.investopedia.com/terms/g/government-grant.asp
- **US Legal**
  http://definitions.uslegal.com/p/public-funds/
- **Ask**
  http://www.ask.com/business-finance/public-funds-72a8a780bc7a3fb3

Grant Funding Takeaways

Understanding the various types of grants and how the varying funding organizations operate, learning how grants from various entities are awarded and/or distributed, and comprehending where these monies come from are very important lessons. No grant, regardless of public or private status, is a shoo-in to receive funding, although many organizations that have been receiving the same grant resources for many years exhibit signs of co-dependency. Such organizations tend to think of the opportunity as a free ride. It's not. Grant awards are not the "end all" to any problem your organization desires to address. They simply assist an organization or organized vehicle/entity in addressing a problem, (possibly) providing solutions, enhancing services, filling gaps, and so forth. All public and private funds, no matter which of them your organization is able to secure, will come with an expiration date. Your organization will always need a rainy day fund plan, or back-up plan for the day when the funding opportunity ceases. A few take away tips for this chapter are listed below:

- Grants are temporary solutions for problems, gaps, and/or needs for various issues or focus areas.

- Each funder (whether private or public) is different. They are as individual and unique as human beings. Some will fund long term, while others are interested in only short-term partnerships.

- Grant funds and grant awards are equally different. Learn as much as possible about each funder from which your organization is interested in making a grant request BEFORE applying for one.

- Just because your organization *can* apply for grant funding from public and private entities does not necessarily mean your organization is *ready* to successfully apply for grants. If you are fairly new to the grant application process, or if you have never applied for grant awards before, visit my website www.getgrantready.com and conduct a free readiness assessment. Do not waste your time applying for grants if your organization is not ready. Funders can spot an ill-prepared applicant like the plague. Regardless of the glowing illustration of your organization written in your application, your organization's secrets, voids, and hidden omissions will be exposed under the scrutiny of an experienced reviewer's eye. So be honest! Let's not even discuss the post-application review process. If your track record isn't non-existent, (some issues in the past may have made the media or the organization has shady staff/board members behaving badly…) it will all be exposed. Readiness is a process within itself. Just do it and save yourself the trouble, embarrassment, and heartache.

- Decide which type of grant you are ready for BEFORE beginning your search. For example, if you have never had a grant award of any type before, you may want to start small with private funders. Because of the amount of reporting and grant management required for public grant funds, your organization may not be ready (or willing) to apply for such grants. Test the waters: start small, pursue private grant awards, and learn the skills necessary to develop sound proposals, get awarded, and implement and report outcomes.

- Do not compare your organization with others similar to your organization (in size or works) and do not believe that, because another local organization receives grants (public or private), your organization should and can qualify for such sources. Again, there are many things taken into consideration when grant funding is awarded. Because your organization is not fully aware of the inner workings of any one particular nonprofit organization, and because your organization may not have access to what was written to make a similar applicant "successful," it is impossible to see why one agency is/was awarded versus another one. Don't assume and don't judge.

- Finally, do not assume finding or writing solid grant proposals is easy. It is quite the contrary, unless you're an excellent story teller. Learning how to find grants is a craft all within itself. It takes a lot of practice and deliberate effort. Grant research is a never ending maze of ups and downs, turns and cliff drops, heartaches and pains, discussions and collaborations, planning and developing, meditation, and phone calls and emails. Grant research is quite time consuming and one must be dedicated to finding funding which meets the needs and focus area(s) of his/her organization. I like to compare looking for a grant like looking for a job—you have to continue until the deal is sealed.

To close, too much information is better than too little. Grant research is a lot like being a private investigator. There is a plethora of information available in the grant-seeking world, free of charge (and additional resources are available for a fee). How to consume this information, where to consume it, and how much to consume is left up to you. The bottom line is that you must start somewhere. Having the proper knowledge about the purposes of grant funding, the eligibility criteria, and the two types of grants (public and private) equates to having half the battle fought and won.

2. HOW TO FIND GRANT FUNDING

Finding grant funding is one of the hardest things for grant-seekers to do. Even if you find *some* grants, finding enough or the *right* grants is very difficult. Well, let me just inform you this is the longest and most informative chapter of this book. Finding grants takes time. It can take years to understand how to find resources because there are so many things that must take place **BEFORE** you begin the search process. There are hundreds, if not thousands, of places to find grant funding opportunities. It takes a significant amount of time to find any type of grant funding opportunities. I'll offer my personal experiences to assist you in developing a format or a selection of methods/process that will enable you to have more fruitful grant research endeavors. Finding someone to give you the important details needed to be successful is difficult; details are usually learned through trial and error. Many grant-writers and researchers don't wish to disclose such information, but it's not mine to hoard. The faster you get this, the faster you can get your first grant award.

Beginning Your Grant Funding Research Endeavors

Before you begin searching for grants, you need to know what you are searching for. By this I mean what does your organization *need*? Do you REALLY know? What is your organization seeking? How much money do you need? Do you have a project outline with a budget already prepared? How soon will you need this funding? Do you have evidence/justification to truly substantiate a need? Do you need board approval prior to drafting proposals? Are you seeking state, federal, or private funding? Do you have the capacity for grant management and compliance? Is the amount of funding your organization is seeking reasonable enough to request from one funder, or will you need to find multiple sources? These are just some of the general questions you need to ask yourself and/or your organization BEFORE seeking grants and grant funders that align with your needs, mission, focus area etc. Doing so makes the process more fruitful, reduces stress, and brings sanity to an activity that can feel like you are in the wild, Wild West all alone. Let me share with you a few processes and filters that I use when searching for grants.

To begin, you must decide WHAT you need grant funding for. Do you need general operating support to help with rent, phone utilities, or administrative salaries? Are you in need of funding to expand or enhance a current or existing program or service? Do you need equipment or furniture? Do you need to hire more staff? Whatever the purpose for seeking grant funding, you will NEED a program/service/project description and a budget—no if, ands, or buts about it. Why must I be so comprehensive in my thought processes? Why are these things so important? You need to align your request with the grant-makers' grant award criteria:

- **Mission Alignment**
  Does your charitable organization's mission match or directly align with that of the grant-maker and the purpose for which they make awards? This is EXTREMELY important when pursuing grant funding. If it does not align, move on and find another grant-maker. Forcing a fit is trouble waiting to happen.

- **Specific Giving Areas**
  Does the funder's grant-making focus areas align with your organization's needs? If it's a state or federal grant, does the funding opportunity announcement align with something your organization currently does or has the ability to do SUCCESSFULLY (key word being <u>successfully</u>).

- **Exemption Status**
Does your organization have the proper exemption status? If your organization is recognized as a tax-exempt organization in the state where the organization's headquarters is located and incorporated, but hasn't completed the IRS tax-exempt status process (which makes the organization a 501 (c) 3 [the public charity status private grant-makers recognize and award]), you may not be eligible to apply for grants at this time. Verify this before applying! Most grant-makers have noted in their charters they only make awards to 501 (c) 3 organizations. Make certain to clarify prior to moving forward with any grant applications.

- **Organizational Good Standing**
Is your organization in good standing with your state's charitable division? Have you filed all of your paperwork and/or reports required annually? Have the proper state charitable organization fees been paid (if applicable)? Have you submitted your organization's most recent 990?[1] Funders will vet your charity to determine whether it meets their funding criteria. The government conducts extensive checks to make sure your organization is compliant with reporting before making awards. Not being in good standing and compliance could prevent you from being awarded. Prepare your organization by exercising due diligence before searching or seeking funding in order to avoid embarrassment.

- **Amount**
Do you know how much funding you need? Is it a reasonable amount? Will you be able to secure this funding from one grant-maker, or will you need several? Do you have a budget that justifies the amount you are requesting? Have you conducted research to determine whether amounts noted within the budget are comparable to similar projects and other organizations locally? Has the amount been agreed upon and finalized by the appropriate agency representatives? Will match be required? Are partners required? Is your request supplanting? Is your proposed request a need, a want, or a hope (because you'll need to substantiate your request, the latter two are unacceptable)? These are some very important things to consider PRIOR to conducting grant research. Some or all of which will need to be hashed out and resolved before beginning a grant research endeavor.

- **Capacity**
Does your organization have the capacity to manage grants and conduct required reporting activities? It is important to determine this information prior to conducting any grant research especially if your organization will be seeking federal and state grant funding opportunities.

Grant Readiness Assessments and Processes

I have created and gathered several items/templates that you will need regarding your grant research activities. These downloadable templates are available at getgrantready.com free of charge. Please take the time to use some of these templates in order to determine what is needed prior to conducting research. The reason for this is that, should the organization or individual responsible for conducting grant research be utilizing a fee-based database for grant research, fine-tuning the search makes a world of difference in the amount of time dedicated to seeking grants. If the grant researcher needs to find funding based on amounts, it helps to know the amount the charity is seeking in order to screen funders

---

[1] An IRS created 990 tax form is used to describe a charitable organization's annual business or operational activities, governance, and detailed financial information and activities. The IRS Form 990 is used by the IRS to determine whether a charity should maintain its tax-exempt status.

that can award the amount needed. If your charity is not in good standing, there is no need for researching and preparing proposals only to find out later that your organization is ineligible. So many questions to ask—so many answers to secure prior to conducting research. These questions may lead to more questions, but at least you have the opportunity to get the ball rolling prior to searching, instead of getting in the middle of the process and getting flustered because these questions haven't been addressed prior to searching. The more refined the search criteria, the less time you waste. It's just that simple. Now, let's discuss how to create a search criteria checklist.

You may create your own or use the simple checklist format below. I am a firm believer in being organized, so I will always offer some type of form, template, or database suggestion throughout the book. I love track records and I love order. Here is a neat little checklist that you could use before beginning each search. I have provided an explanation section as well for the template:

Basic Funding Search Checklist Template

Grant-seeking Criteria	Response
Name Project/Program/Service:	
Total Amount of Funding Sought:	
Timeline of Need:	
Specific Items Needed:	
Defined Focus Area(s):	
Type of Grant Funding:	

Explanations

Grant-seeking Criteria	Explanation
Name Project/Program/Service:	Information in this section will help you stay focused and guide you to funders aligned with your response or request.
Total Amount of Funding Sought:	Information is needed to help you find funders that fund only what you need.
Timeline of Need:	Information is needed to determine how soon funding is needed. Short-term, mid-term, or long-term ranges can be used, or you can simply indicate a time or quarter of any specific year. You should start with a 6-9 month goal (short-term).
Specific Items Needed:	Having a short (or long) list of items that you are attempting to secure funding for is very helpful. The reason being that some funders may not fund your entire request. You may need to break your single request into several mini requests in order to

	secure funding for an entire project/program/service/or activity. You may have to change your thought processes in order to meet your financial goal.
Defined Focus Area(s):	Defining the specific focus area of all requests is quite helpful when using electronic databases for grant funding searches. Keywords are so much more effective and will ensure you get the most information out of an individual search. Remember, you may search for days (even weeks) on one topic, so be thoughtful, clear, and concise with key words and how they relate to your grant funding needs.
Type of Grant Funding:	Are you seeking federal, state, or private foundation grant funding? This is necessary to refine searches. There are sites to search specifically for federal funding. There are also sites that assist with searches regarding private grant-making foundations. If you will have a combination, then it is still necessary to clearly define this to stay on task and to make sure your needs are matched with the funding type.

Now that you have a sample mini-template to model for future searches, it's time to move on to the next area: where to find funding. There are a number of ways to find grant funding resources. A simple Google search will yield you a few results, but not as many as you would like/need. It is more effective to find grant resources based on the type (i.e. public versus private). Let's start with the public (state and federal) grant funding resources first.

Public grant resource appropriations can be found for every state and U.S. Territory. You may find these public grant funding opportunities via each state's individual public agency itself (e.g. Office of Public Health, State Department of Education, Department of Health and Environmental Control, Department of Health and Human Services). There are literally too many state agencies to find and name (if I tried, I would never be able to finish this book). If you would like to seek state public grants by a particular agency, I suggest conducting a search simply titled "(Name of the State) grants." You should at least get a listing of state agencies with grant-making capacities with which you may begin. Again, with so many state entities across America; you could spend over a year finding out what is available. Starting a state search is the best option available at this point. You may also check with you public library to ask if your state has amassed a resource guide or two that can assist with researching state grant funding opportunities.

State Public Grant Funding and Resources

To learn more about your state budget, or if you have any questions or concerns, you should inquire with your state's budget office. When pursing state funding, keeping abreast of past and current state and federal legislation as well as annual budget appropriations is very important. To find your state's budget office, conduct a simple Google search. You may also visit the National Association of Budget Offices' website[2], where information (including web addresses), is provided for the budget offices for all 50 states and U.S. Territories. Because each site may use varying terminology and labeling for the sections you need to pursue, utilize keywords such as transparency, citizen services, appropriations, bills, legislation, state budget, state spending, procurement, state salaries, and grants. I would spend a great quantity of time navigating the site for your state to learn more about how to find the information relative to *your* state, *your* questions, and *your* needs. This process will also be helpful for national grant-writers. Being able to stay abreast of state appropriations and opportunities is great for collaborative partnership alignments.

State Budget Office	Website
Alabama	http://budget.alabama.gov
Alaska	http://omb.alaska.gov
Arizona	http://www.ospb.state.az.us
California	http://www.ospb.state.az.us
Connecticut	http://www.ct.gov/opm/site/default.asp
Delaware	http://omb.delaware.gov/default.shtml
Florida	http://www.flgov.com/opb
Georgia	http://opb.georgia.gov
Hawaii	http://budget.hawaii.gov
Idaho	http://dfm.idaho.gov
Illinois	http://www.state.il.us/budget
Indiana	http://www.in.gov/sba
Iowa	http://www.dom.state.ia.us
Kansas	http://budget.ks.gov/
Kentucky	http://www.osbd.ky.gov/default
Louisiana	http://www.doa.louisiana.gov/opb/index.htm
Maine	http://www.state.me.us/budget
Maryland	http://dbm.maryland.gov/Pages/home.aspx
Massachusetts	http://www.mass.gov/anf
Michigan	http://www.michigan.gov/budget
Minnesota	http://www.mmb.state.mn.us
Missouri	http://oa.mo.gov/bp/
Montana	http://www.budget.mt.gov/default.mcpx
Nebraska	http://budget.ne.gov/
Nevada	http://budget.nv.gov
New Hampshire	http://admin.state.nh.us/budget
New Jersey	http://www.state.nj.us/treasury/omb/

---

[2] http://www.nasbo.org/resources/state-budget-office-directory

New Mexico	http://www.nmdfa.state.nm.us/
New York	http://www.budget.ny.gov/
North Carolina	http://www.osbm.state.nc.us
North Dakota	http://www.nd.gov/omb/
Ohio	http://obm.ohio.gov/
Oklahoma	http://ok.gov/OSF/
Oregon	http://www.bam.das.state.or.us/
Pennsylvania	http://www.budget.state.pa.us
Rhode Island	http://www.budget.state.ri.us/
South Carolina	http://www.admin.sc.gov/budget
South Dakota	http://bfm.sd.gov/
Tennessee	http://www.tn.gov/finance/bud/budget.shtml
Texas	http://governor.state.tx.us/bpp
Utah	http://www.governor.utah.gov/gopb/
Vermont	http://finance.vermont.gov/
Virginia	http://dpb.virginia.gov/
Washington	http://www.ofm.wa.gov/
West Virginia	http://www.budget.wv.gov/Pages/default.aspx
Wisconsin	http://www.doa.state.wi.us/Home
Wyoming	http://ai.state.wy.us/budget/
American Samoa	http://americansamoa.gov/?page=opb
District of Columbia	http://cfo.dc.gov/
Guam	http://bbmr.guam.gov/
Puerto Rico	http://www.ogp.gobierno.pr/
Virgin Islands	http://finance.gov.vg/Economy/

Before moving on to federal grant resources and funding, let me mention one last note. Be sure to, when utilizing online resources, rely on sites ending in ".org" versus ".com." Dot com or ".com" sites usually are for-profit sites and most will provide some misleading information related to grants in some (or all) 50 states. I'm not unsupportive of the use of those sites for potential leads. I just don't want you to get sucked into any gimmicks that will only yield heartache and pain. Those sites may also leave you feeling jilted if you spend any money hoping to gain "additional" information. Most public grant-making agencies provide some type of formal notice of funding availability, funding opportunity announcements, and so forth via online solicitations to the public free of charge. You can secure this information by phone or through a public search. If you decide to pay for any information pertaining to any public grant funding opportunity, then you have the right to do so. You should know up front, though, that you do not have to. It may be the easiest route, but not the wisest. Happy state grant funding hunting!

Federal Public Grant Funding Resources

Now, let's move on to federal grant resources. Federal grant resources are a lot easier to locate. The federal government does an amazing job at creating methods for disseminating information related to federal grant funding opportunities.

The Federal Register: https://www.federalregister.gov/agencies

The Federal Register is a daily chronicling of the United States Government. This site contains information and documents that are applicable to the general public including notices of public meetings, hearings, investigations, grants and funding, environmental impact statements, information collections, statements of organization and functions, delegations, and other announcements of public interest. Every grant announcement by any federal agency can be found here. You can search this site by public agency and search recently released funding opportunity announcements (FOAs). You may also sign up for alerts for daily Federal Register Digest notifications.

Grants.Gov: http://www.grants.gov/web/grants/home.html

Grants.gov is a one-stop shop where grant-seekers can find and apply for any federal grant funding opportunities (competitive and non-competitive). Grant-seekers can sign up for various grant alerts, review tutorials on federal grant-writing, and learn about all of the federal grant-making agencies, grant policies, grant fraud, the online submission process, registering as an authorized organizational representative (which allows designated individuals to submit proposals on behalf of your nonprofit organization or governmental agency), determine agency and grant eligibility, and more.

Catalog of Federal Domestic Assistance (CFDA):
https://www.cfda.gov/

The Catalog of Federal Domestic Assistance (CFDA) provides a full listing of all federal programs available to state and local governments (including the District of Columbia), federally recognized Indian tribal governments, territories (and possessions) of the United States, domestic public, quasi-public, and private profit and nonprofit organizations and institutions, specialized groups, and individuals. The Catalog of Federal Domestic Assistance is a government-wide compendium of Federal programs, projects, services, and activities that provides assistance or benefits to the American public. It contains both financial and nonfinancial assistance programs administered by federal departments and establishments of the federal government.

This is merely a synopsis of federal grant sites that function as sort of clearinghouses for all things federal grant funding related. Now, we will discuss the various federal agencies. There are a large number of federal, grant-making agencies within the federal government. Hundreds of offices and programs underneath each federal agency release grant funding opportunities. You may register with each individual grant funding agency to receive federal grant funding announcements as they are released.

Below is a list of every federal, grant-making agency, the number of programs under each federal agency's umbrella, and the agency's website. Visit each website in order to learn more about the agency's purpose and register (where applicable) for updates on potential funding opportunities.

Federal Agency	Number of Offices	Number of Programs	Website
Agency for International Development	0	12	www.usaid.gov
Appalachian Regional			

Agency			Website
Commission	0	5	www.arc.gov
Architectural and Transportation Barriers Compliance Board	0	1	www.access-board.gov/
Barry Goldwater Scholarship and Excellence In Education Foundation	0	1	goldwater.scholarsapply.org/
Broadcasting Board of Governors	0	1	www.bbg.gov
Christopher Columbus Fellowship Foundation	0	3	www.christophercolumbusfoundation.gov/
Corporation for National and Community Service	0	15	www.nationalservice.gov/
Delta Regional Authority	0	3	www.dra.gov
Denali Commission	0	1	www.denali.gov
Department of Agriculture	18	268	www.usda.gov
Department of Commerce	12	93	www.commerce.gov
Department of Defense	26	86	www.defense.gov
Department of Education	13	120	www.ed.gov
Department of Energy	0	35	energy.gov
Department of Health and Human Services	19	523	www.hhs.gov
Department of Homeland Security	0	82	www.dhs.gov
Department of Housing and Urban Development	7	115	portal.hud.gov or www.hud.gov/funds/index.cfm
Department of Justice	21	136	www.justice.gov
Department of Labor	14	60	www.dol.gov
Department of State	38	70	www.state.gov
Department of the Interior	16	272	www.doi.gov
Department of the Treasury	5	11	www.treasury.gov
Department of Transportation	12	90	www.transportation.gov
Department of Veterans Affairs	3	63	www.va.gov
Executive Office of			www.whitehouse.gov/administration/eop

the President	0	6	www.usa.gov
Federal Mediation and Conciliation Service	0	2	www.fmcs.gov/internet/
Gulf Coast Ecosystem Restoration Council	0	2	www.restorethegulf.gov/
Harry S Truman Scholarship Foundation	0	1	www.truman.gov
Institute of Museum and Library Services	0	7	www.imls.gov
James Madison Memorial Fellowship Foundation	0	1	www.jamesmadison.gov
Japan U.S. Friendship Commission	0	1	www.jusfc.gov
Millennium Challenge Corporation	0	2	www.mcc.gov
Morris K. Udall Foundation	0	2	udall.gov
National Aeronautics and Space Administration (NASA)	0	12	www.nasa.gov
National Archives and Records Administration	0	2	www.archives.gov
National Credit Union Administration	0	1	www.ncua.gov
National Endowment for the Arts	0	2	arts.gov
National Endowment for the Humanities	0	9	www.neh.gov
National Science Foundation	0	13	www.nsf.gov
Northern Border Regional Commission	0	1	northernforest.org
Nuclear Regulatory Commission	0	4	www.nrc.gov
Peace Corps	0	1	www.peacecorps.gov
Small Business Administration	0	25	www.sba.gov
Smithsonian Institution	0	1	www.si.edu
Social Security Administration	0	9	www.ssa.gov
U.S. Election Assistance Commission	0	4	www.eac.gov

United States Institute of Peace	0	4	www.usip.org
Vietnam Education Foundation	0	4	home.vef.gov
Woodrow Wilson International Center for Scholars	0	1	www.loc.gov
Side Notes			
Some programs (such as NIH, Office of Postsecondary of Education, and Office of Family Assistance) are located under the umbrella of the U.S. Department of Health and Human Services. You will need to learn which programs and offices are located under which federal agency. Each federal agency has similar grant-making offices and programs under its umbrella. This will enable you to follow grant funding decisions in the future as it relates to federal legislation. Also, note that there are 68 federal agencies. Not all are noted in this table, as some of the offices do not award grants. They have other jobs, such as oversight, technical assistance, loan programs, and information dissemination. Finally, not all programs noted in this table are grant-making programs. Please visit the Catalog of Federal Domestic Assistance[3] to learn more about each agency, the specific programs operating within those federal agencies, and the specific types of opportunities that may be of interest to your organization. I encourage you to get to know your government and learn how your tax dollars work.			

The Different Types of Federal Grants

When searching for federal grants, you will see there are MANY types of grants: formula, congressionally directed awards, discretionary grants, project grants, cooperative agreements, and payment programs. Some agencies, such as the National Institute of Health, have even more grant types. Be sure to research the agency's grant awarding formulas. There is a lot to learn here, and knowledge is power. The following are the basic grant types that grant-seekers will likely attempt to secure through grant proposal development efforts:

- **Formula grants** are funding programs that you do not compete for, even though you must submit an application and meet other specified requirements. Usually administered and managed by State Administering Agencies, they ensure that designated recipients will receive funds.

- **Congressionally Directed Awards** are directed awards, or earmarks, that direct approved funds to be spent on specific projects or direct specific exemptions from taxes or mandated fees. Congressionally directed awards do not mandate additional government spending, but rather allocate approved spending for specific purposes. Congressionally directed awards can be satisfied through either a grant or a cooperative agreement.

- **Discretionary Grants** are awarded directly by federal programs to eligible recipients, usually on a competitive basis. Applications undergo a preliminary review process to ensure that the are complete and meet the eligibility requirements.

- **Payment Programs** fund participating jurisdictions for designated purposes, but do not involve post-award activities.

---

[3] www.cfda.gov/agencies

- **Project Grants** are grants meant for fixed or known periods of specific projects. Project grants can include fellowships, scholarships, research grants, training grants, traineeships, experimental and demonstration grants, evaluation grants, planning grants, technical assistance grants, survey grants, and construction grants.

Using Keywords to Conduct Federal Funding Grant Searches

Next, you will need to know where to search for federal grant funding, depending on the work your organization does and the type of funding you are pursuing. This can be somewhat complicated because some agencies have many programs that offer various types of grant awards. For example, the U.S. Department of Education may offer School Resource Officer grants via a program/office called the Office of Elementary and Secondary Education because that is one of the offices responsible for school security at some level. Depending on how your state/region/locale is set up, your school district may have it covered, but the county or city may cover this expense. There's a possibility that law enforcement works in collaboration with the school district, county, and state to cover School Resource Officer salaries and expenses. In any event, I could use hundreds of other examples to demonstrate how complicated searching for grant funding can become. I created a sample keyword agency link table as a demonstration of how you will need to think outside of the box when searching for funding opportunities.

**Helpful Hint*: Consider including the numerous aspects you're search for: partners, specific items needed, the focus area(s) (e.g. education, law enforcement, first responders, family assistance, human services, science, research, college preparation).

Keyword	Potential Federal Funding Agency/Program
Law Enforcement, First Responders, Police, Sheriff, National Security	FEMA, U.S. Department of Justice, Office of Justice Programs, COPS, Bureau of Justice Assistance, Homeland Security, U.S. Department of Transportation
Child Abuse and Neglect, Foster Children	U.S. Department of Health and Human Services—Office of Family Services, Children's Bureau
Community Economic Development, Workforce Development	U.S. Department of Health & Human Services—Office of Community Economic Development, National Credit Union Administration
Human Services, Child Care, Medicare, Respite, Rural Health	U.S. Department of Health and Human Services
Education, College, Special Education, STEMS	National Science Foundation, U.S. Department of Education—Office of Postsecondary Education
Business Innovation, Research	Small Business Administration and National Institutes of Health—Small Business Innovation Research

These are just *some* examples of federal funding sources to assist you in thinking of ways to connect your funding needs with a federal funding source. Let me reiterate: there are a variety of ways to connect these dots. You'll need to work to find a method that works for you. We learn differently, so find the method that suits your needs and makes you comfortable. We have covered where to search for federal grant funding, now let's move on to private *(foundation)* grant funding.

Obtaining Hard Copy Private Funding Resources for Research

There are hundreds of methods and places to search for grant funding. I'll spend a significant amount of time explaining this area. My goal is to help you be successful in finding great opportunities for your organization. Let's start with hard copy resources first. There are very few hard copy resources available to purchase that will provide you with a plethora of private foundations. Because there are so many foundations, and because the information is readily available (though not easily found) online, it is easier to refer grant-seekers to online resources. The few hard copy items I found that may be of use are noted below:

- "**21st Century Master Guide to Private Foundations and Federal Grant Programs**"
  Thousands of Funding Sources DVD-Rom Set
  Amazon.com—$22.95
- "**The Foundation Center's Celebrity Foundation Directory**"
  2009 Edition
  Foundationcenter.org—$59.95
- "**The Foundation Center's Guide to Funding for International and Foreign Programs**"
  11th edition
  Foundationcenter.org—$125 (or $350 for the entire series)
- "**The Foundation Center's Digital Guides available in 15 subject areas**
  Includes the arts, health, and religion
  2015 Editions
  Foundationcenter.org—$39.95 (Single Edition Guides)

I strongly recommend purchasing hard copy publications for several reasons:

- **The information rarely changes.** Foundations either cease operating, change focuses, change leadership, or decrease or increase in assets annually. Because there are so few changes, it doesn't make any sense to pay for annual online grant prospecting subscriptions for information all year long when you can simply pay a one-time fee to purchase hard copy or digital materials. Board members may change, web addresses may change, but the majority of a private foundation's corporate information rarely changes, making the idea of utilizing hard copy resources to locate funders an attractive alternative to monthly online subscriptions.
- **You never have to worry about ongoing fees.** Fees are one and done. With online subscriptions, you may get varied prices for various levels of access. Once you buy a complete resource directory, you're done. You have it and it's yours. It's a smarter investment. Should your organization become strapped for cash and need to cut back on expenses, these are already paid for. Used in concert with the internet, you get the same results.

- **Legacy.** Organizations that invest in such resources for their agencies always have resources to use in the event where there is high staff turnover or new people are assigned to grant proposal development tasks. Should the organization utilize interns and/or volunteers, then there are hard copy publications that can be used onsite, enabling research to continue.

- **Resources are available 24-7.** On the go and your computer runs out of battery power while conducting online search or you need to travel? Carry your hard copy grant resource guides with you. No internet? Hard copy grant funding prospecting resources don't require internet access. No money to pay for high priced subscriptions? No worries! Your hard copy guides is available 24-7, regardless of the internet service.

- **All of your information is in one place.** When using electronic databases and conducting your own online searches, the options are never ending, exhausting, and (at times) frustrating. By purchasing hard copy grant publications you will have the information by focus area, in your hands, in one place.

Hard Copy Resources

Although you may decide to purchase hard copy resources, you will still utilize online resources to verify information discovered during a hard copy inquiry. Hopefully, some of the justifications noted above will help in your decisions regarding the benefits of hard copy grant guide resources. I purchased hard copy guides nearly 11 years ago and I still use them. To me, they are lifesavers.

Before I move on to online resources, let's spend some time on other locations to find potential resources. There are a number of types of resources and places to search for hard copy/pdf publication grant resources.

Public Libraries
The Chronicle of Philanthropy
Nonprofit Times
The Chronicle of Higher Education
Society for Nonprofits

The Aspen Institute
Philanthropy.com
Nonprofit Quarterly
Stanford Social Innovation Review
Philanthropy News Digest

Again, so many resources are available online for purchase that you should have no problem in finding several to meet your prospecting needs. Please take your time and review trade journals, magazines, periodicals, newspapers, and newsletters for resources beneficial to your resource needs. Now, let's move on to discover online grant prospecting databases.

Online Private Grant Research Resources (Free and Fee-Per-Use)

Online grant directory databases offer access to nearly 700,000 private foundations in the U.S. Utilizing online grant prospecting resources has many benefits. There are hundreds of sites that provide access to private funding grant opportunities. Some are very good, comprehensive, and relative, while other databases offer very few details. At the end of the day, even if you decide to utilize an online database for finding the initial potential source of funding, you will still need to verify and cross-verify the information you gather from any electronic database. The reason being, things change. Private foundations make decisions to change foundation operations every single day. Some of these changes are miniscule and irrelevant to grant-seekers, such as board meetings and other legal matters. But some of the changes are extremely important to grant-seekers, enabling them to make informed decisions about proposal development and submissions. The following are details that should be researched thoroughly and frequently:

- **Focus Areas/Priorities:** Make sure each foundation hasn't changed focus areas or "giving" priorities.

- **Operations/Grant-Making:** Make certain that the foundation hasn't ceased operations or put grant-making on hold until they have hashed out a new direction. Sometimes, foundations cease operations or wind down because they have used all of their assets, fulfilling the purpose, mission, and vision of the founders. In some instances, misfortunes (such as the Bernie Madoff scandal[4]) wipe out the assets of foundations.

- **Grant Award Ranges:** Grant award ranges may increase or decrease at any time, based on a foundation's assets.

- **Address Changes:** Funders may move offices or relocate headquarters to new states. So, mail-in proposals (hard copy grant proposals) may need to be submitted to new mailing addresses. Knowing where to send a proposal or inquiry may determine whether your proposal is funded.

- **Application Processes:** More and more funders are switching to online application processes with those dreaded boxes that count characters. Application submission deadlines/dates change. Application formatting (e.g. page numbers) may be altered. Always check for the most recent information—and check often.

- **Reviewing Assets/Annual Reports:** Check 990-PF returns and private foundation annual reports often to ensure that assets and leadership haven't been significantly changed.

- **Leadership Changes:** Turnovers, Program Officer Changes, etc. happen frequently at private foundations. It is always good to make sure all correspondence reaches the appropriate contact person.

Now that we have discussed the reasons for conducting additional searches, let's move on to those online grant funder databases. The information found on some of these databases may vary, but all of the information is relevant. I do not have any particular preference for any specific database and I have not used/tested all of the databases. I have researched these sites to ensure the actual links work. You will have the ability to make informed decisions about each of them.

One Final Note

Please, please, *please*, don't let any website or database sway you by saying they are "the best" or "the leading." The only way you will ever know what is best for you is to try them out for yourself. Some sites are easy to use, some have more information, and some target specific focus areas. Pick what's best for you. I always prefer free over a membership subscription fee, but I have been at this for some time and I have compiled a great number of resources. Your time, needs, and ability (or inability) to pay for short-term and/or long-term membership fees are the only important issues. If all else fails, colleges and libraries (public resources) are great places to start looking for free resources.

Grant Database Name/Site * Fee Required to Use	Web Address

---

[4] Bernie Madoff, the former Chairman of the NASDAQ, confessed and was convicted of running a large Ponzi scheme, losing about 50 billion dollars of his clients' money. Clients included celebrities, a number of nonprofits, and private grant-making foundations. (http://www.biography.com/people/bernard-madoff-466366)

1. *Grant Station	www.grantstation.com
2. *Chronicle of Philanthropy	www.philanthropy.com/
3. *Funds Net	www.fundsnetservices.com
4. *Grant Gopher	www.grantgopher.com
5. *Grant Watch	www.grantwatch.com
6. *Grant Select	www.grantselect.com/
7. *Grant Vine	www.grantvine.net
8. *Foundation Directory Online	www.fconline.foundationcenter.org/
9. The Grantsmanship Center	www.tgci.com/funding-sources
10. *Big Online America	www.bigdatabase.com
11. Houghton Mifflin Court	www.hmhco.com
12. *Foundation Search	www.foundationsearch.com/
13. Council on Foundations	www.cof.org
14. *Guidestar	www.guidestar.org/
15. Nozasearch	www.nozasearch.com
16. Stanford School of Medicine	www.med.stanford.edu/rmg/funding/funding_database.html
17. *Police Grants	www.policeone.com/grants/
18. Fundsnet.com	http://www.fundsnetservices.com
19. Power of Discovery	www.powerofdiscovery.org/grant_databases
20. Grant Wrangler	http://grantwrangler.com/
21. Discount School Supply	www.discountschoolsupply.com/Community/Grants.aspx
22. Texas Department of State Health Services	www.dshs.state.tx.us/fic/search.asp
23. University of Wisconsin	http://libraryguides.uwsp.edu/content.php?pid=171998&sid=1449427
24. Grant Forward	www.grantforward.com/index
25. University of North Carolina Chapel Hill	baileydemofundingportal.web.unc.edu/funding-databases/
26. Sierra Nevada Conservancy	www.sierranevada.ca.gov/other-assistance/searchable-grants-database
27. School Funding Center	www.schoolfundingcenter.info/
28. EDinformatics	www.edinformatics.com/grant_agencies/
29. California Educational Collaborative	http://cccetc.org/grants/databases.php
30. U.S. Environmental Protection Agency	www2.epa.gov/home/grants-and-other-funding-opportunities
31. Pivot	http://pivot.cos.com/
32. Grant Gate	http://grantgate.com/
33. University of Northern Colorado	www.unco.edu/osp/funding/external/databases.html
34. Federal Funds for States	www.ffis.org/database
35. Thomas Jefferson University	http://jeffline.tju.edu/Researchers/grants/funded-gov.html
36. Foundation Grants	www.foundation-grants.com/
37. National Science Foundation	www.nsf.gov/funding/
38. Center for Nonprofit Excellence	www.cnpe.org
39. Grantmakers for Education	edfunders.org/our-community/member-organizations

40. Research Professional	info.researchprofessional.com/
41. Top 100 Private Foundations	foundationcenter.org/findfunders/topfunders/top100assets.html
42. National Center for Charitable Statistics	http://nccs.urban.org/

Don't forget to conduct research on your favorite corporations—or any corporation, for that matter: Walmart, Tommy Hilfiger, Chicos, Applebees, Chili's, Ben & Jerry's Ice Cream, Firestone Tire Company, Kohls Department Stores, Macy's Target, Charles Schwab, Bank of America, Wells Fargo, Hallmark Cards, professional sports teams (football, basketball, baseball), restaurant franchises, etc. The list can go on forever and a day. Survey your community to see what types of large national or regional corporations (businesses) are located in your area. Some may have more opportunities for grant awards than others, but it's a much easier way to find grant funding than dissecting online databases. Please be aware that some private grant-making corporations have very specific geographical focus areas. Read the guidelines carefully and, when in doubt, email or make a phone call.

Also, don't forget about your local community foundations. Every state usually has some type of resource directory where one can easily access information about community grant-making foundations. If not, visit your local library to discover what options are available to assist you in your research endeavors. This is the most difficult part of grant-writing: finding a grant funder in the first place. Be patient. Be diligent. Be resourceful. Use your time wisely and begin thinking outside of the box. Also, don't hesitate to contact local or regional United Ways or community foundations to inquire about potential grant funding prospects. They are excellent leads to cultivating new relationships.

3. COMMUNITY AND TARGET POPULATION RESEARCH

If I have not reiterated the importance of research before, let me do so now. Research is so very important as it relates to the grant-writing world. However, researching grant funding opportunities is only one part of this technical process. The next component of the research process is understanding the problem(s) for which you are seeking funding. By understanding the problem, I am referring to being able to clearly, concisely, and definitively describe the problem that your organization is seeking to address. As a grant reviewer, I can tell you that, if you cannot illustrate that you have a need or provide a compelling argument that a problem truly exists, you will be unable to develop an effective approach as a solution to the problem for which you seek funding. There are so many different things varying grant funders are seeking when asking grant-seekers for a "Statement of Need" or a "Problem Statement." Your response will depend on page limits, character limits, and the audience (public funding grant-maker vs. private funding grant-maker). There is coded language in grant proposal criteria and solicitations. You will need to understand the code in order to provide the appropriate responses. This code needs to be deciphered and this chapter will assist you.

Some Context Regarding the Grant Proposal Review Process (After Submission)

In my opinion, the best way to learn how to understand what your community's needs are and how to formulate a valid assessment that you are able to share in a complete manner is to use a federal funding opportunity announcement's needs section. Although private funders may not require the comprehensiveness of the federal application, the section will provide you with an idea of how to prepare a statement of need that is comprehensive enough to convincingly illustrate the problem. I will use some language from federal funding opportunity announcements, provide you with the appropriate information that should be contained in each section, and share with you the sources where grant proposal developers will need to go to collect this information (data).

Proposals are reviewed objectively by persons coming from a variety of educational and professional backgrounds, careers, states and regions of the United States, and personal experiences. When grant reviewers (also known as peer reviewers, panel reviewers, or objective reviewers) review federal, state, and private proposals, they use their expertise to assess whether applications are worthy to be funded based on the criteria and guidance provided by the funder. These grant proposal reviewers come from a variety of backgrounds and from all 50 states, including U.S. territories. Federal legislation requires such diversity to attain the most objective peer reviews. Private foundations set their own application processes, but most foundations, in an effort to avoid bias, attempt to recruit community volunteers to read grant proposals. I share this with you because you need to understand that the quality of your research will most certainly dictate the score your proposal receives as well as whether or not your proposals receive funding. You must understand the following concerning research and why it is so vital that you conduct thorough assessments and research.

- Reviewers likely will not be from your state, as they may be from all over the nation. A federal reviewer from Florida may review proposals from Washington State, as they will have absolutely no earthly idea about your needs, your issues, your target population, and/or your community. Your research must provide reviewers with enough information to assess need. A shallow or incomplete search will lead to a downgrade in your application. Take no chances; be thorough. Great research provides context for grant proposal reviewers.

- Take the time to read sample partial criteria. A description from a federal funding opportunity announcement can be found below. The criteria may be worded differently from private foundation criteria.

Criteria: Statement of Need, Need for Assistance, Demonstration of Need
(1) Clearly identify the physical, economic, social, financial, institutional, and/or other problem(s) requiring a solution.
(2) The need for assistance, including the nature and scope of the problem, must be demonstrated and the principal and subordinate objectives of the project must be clearly and concisely stated. Supporting documentation, such as letters of support and testimonials from concerned interests other than the applicant, may be included.
(3) Any relevant data based on planning studies should be included or referred to in the endnotes/footnotes.
(4) Incorporate demographic data and participant/beneficiary information as well as data describing the needs of the target population and the proposed service area as needed.
(5) When appropriate, a literature review[1] should be used to support the objectives and needs described in this section.

Let me clearly dissect each sentence of the criteria to help you understand how important this information is and why.

Sample Criteria	**What Proposal Reviewers Are Seeking (Definition)**
Criteria 1.) Clearly identify the physical, economic, social, financial, institutional, and/or other problem(s) requiring a solution.	Proposal reviewers will be in search of information such as poverty rates, number of low-income households, percentage of high school and college graduates in the area, crime rates, target/service areas, racial/ethnic data, age groups, school data (free and reduced lunch, progression rates), housing information (rent vs. own), and any other data related to your problem (e.g. incarceration rates, single-parent households, juvenile delinquency issues, number of seniors in the area, well-being). Data and information should be as up-to-date as possible, being no greater than three years old. If you are unable to find data for a specific area, please specify this as well as any reason you decide to use data greater than three years old.
Criteria 2.) The need for assistance, including the nature and scope of the problem, must be demonstrated.	This is where you describe the actual problem. Here, "bad is good," so let it rip. Describe the problem which creates the organization's needs.
Criteria 3.) Any relevant data based on planning studies should be included or referred to in the endnotes/footnotes.	Reviewers will be looking for evidence-based studies and other relevant (and reliable) articles or publications—local information on focus groups previously conducted, institutional studies, etc. If using multiple sources or references, be sure to cite them all.
Criteria 4.) Incorporate	Address this criteria in the same manner that you would criteria

---

[1] A literary review is a critical analysis of a published body of knowledge through summary, classification, and comparison of prior research studies, reviews of literature, and theoretical articles.

demographic data and participant/beneficiary information as well as data describing the needs of the target population and the proposed service area as needed.	#1. If you are going to be helping people, then the data you need to provide must be about the people and area you intend to serve. Data provides context for reviewers. They may know nothing about your target area or population. Educate your readers as much as possible.
Criteria 5.) When appropriate, a literature review should be used to support the objectives and needs described in this section.	When conducting research, you may find an evidence-based reference or a published journal with information, science, studies, etc. that helps prove your need for assistance; be sure to cite the sources in the manner the funder requests. When in doubt, ask.

This is only one example of many different types of criteria that a grant-writer may possibly encounter. I use this criteria because it will give you a chance to collect the most comprehensive description of need that you could possibly develop. I strongly recommend that you use this criteria to develop a full assessment of the people or area(s) that an agency serves. I know that different agencies will be writing for different purposes, so this criteria may need to be modified in order to assist you with your specific research efforts. At times, you may need to read a funder's criteria several times to gain more understanding about exactly what it is they are seeking from an applicant. I have read hundreds of solicitations and find some (literally) impossible to understand. I tend to overthink at times, wanting to make sure I provide as much information as possible. I find it helps to walk away for a day or two and review the solicitation criteria again with a fresh pair of eyes (and a rested brain). Most of the time, this helps. When all else fails, ask a couple of different people to read the criteria with which you may be having issues. Although their interpretation may be completely different, it could help bring clarity. Now, let's move on to places to assist with your criteria research.

Narrative/Grant Proposal Research Resources and Sites

There are a number places where you may conduct a variety of research related to anything you will ever need in order to inform funders about your needs. Below are all the sources I use (or have used in the past). For each data or informational source, I list a brief description of how the resource may be useful in your research efforts.

Data/Information Source	Purpose
Atlas of Rural and Small Town America http://www.ers.usda.gov/data-products/atlas-of-rural-and-small-town-america.aspx	Contains socioeconomic data related to rural communities in America
Census Data Quick Facts http://quickfacts.census.gov/qfd/index.html	Provides quick U.S. Census Data facts regarding any state, county, or U.S. Territory
Census Bureau (U.S.) http://www.census.gov	Provides an array of data including maps, tables, and a more comprehensive look at state, towns, counties, unincorporated communities, etc.
Best Places http://www.bestplaces.net/	Analyzes information on the cost of living, community crime rates, home prices, city rankings, best

	places, etc.
Bureau of Justice Statistics http://www.bjs.gov/	One-stop shop for crime, court, prison, jail, and arrest data (Some agencies do not report crime data.)
Bureau of Transportation Statistics http://www.rita.dot.gov/bts/home	State and national statistics related to most modes of transportation
Census Scope http://censusscope.org/	An easy to use tracking tool, pulling information from the U.S. Census Bureau
Child Trends Data Bank http://www.childtrends.org/databank/	Dedicated to all statistics and information related to the well-being of children and to the monitoring of over 100 indicators that focus on risks and positive development of children and youth
CIA World Book www.cia.gov/library/publications/the-world-factbook	Provides information and statistics about every country, dependency, and geographic entity in the world
Economic Statistics Briefing Room http://www.census.gov/economic-indicators/	National, state, and local economic wellness indicators and other data related to the economy
Education Statistics http://nces.ed.gov/	Primary federal entity for collecting and analyzing data related to education
The Education Trust http://edtrust.org/	Provides reports, students, and policy information related to the state of public education in the U.S.
Empowerment Zones, Federal (HUD) http://egis.hud.gov/ezrclocator/	Information on federal empowerment zones, enterprise communities, enterprise zones, and renewal communities
ESRI (fee for use may be required for site) http://www.esri.com/about-esri	Provides information regarding how geography affects crime, traffic safety, home foreclosures, urban planning, resource management, emergency services, marketing, and the environment
Federal Interagency Forum on Child and Family Statistics http://www.childstats.gov/	A collection of 22 Federal government agencies involved in research and activities related to children and families
Fed Stats http://fedstats.sites.usa.gov/	Federal data from more than 100 agencies on topics like economic and population trends, crime, education, health care, aviation safety, energy use, farm production and more
FirstGov	Any array of state, local, and

http://firstgov.gov.com/	federal information from a variety of sources (anything government related)
Free Lunch https://www.economy.com/freelunch/	Free economic, demographic, and financial data
Great Schools http://www.greatschools.org/	Public and private school comparison data
Inter-University Consortium for Political and Social Research http://www.icpsr.umich.edu/icpsrweb/ICPSR/index.jsp	Data archive of more than 500,000 files of research in the social sciences with 16 specialized collections of data in education, aging, criminal justice, substance abuse, terrorism, and other fields
International Statistics http://www.census.gov/compendia/statab/cats/international **(Transportation)** http://www.rita.dot.gov/bts/sites/rita.dot.gov.bts/files/subject_areas/international/index.html **(United Nations Statistics Division)** http://unstats.un.org/unsd/methods/inter-natlinks/sd_intstat.htm **(International Energy Agency)** http://www.iea.org/statistics/ **(Bureau of Labor of Statistics)** http://www.bls.gov/bls/other.htm **(World Statistics)** http://world-statistics.org/ **(International Justice Statistics)** http://www.bjs.gov/content/ijs.cfm	International statistics and information on a variety of topics
Kids Count Data Center http://datacenter.kidscount.org/	Data on child and family well-being in the United States (allows you to download data and create reports and graphics)
National Agricultural Statistics Services http://www.nass.usda.gov/Data_and_Statistics/index.asp	Agricultural statistics for every state and county in the United States
National Assessment of Adult Literacy (NAAL) http://nces.ed.gov/naal/index.asp	Data and information regarding adult literacy educational attainment rates in the United States.
National Association of Counties http://www.naco.org/Pages/default.aspx	Information related to county governments in the United States
National Atlas of the United States http://nationalmap.gov/small_scale/atlasftp.html	Maps of all sorts, downloadable for imbedding in your grant proposals (assists with demonstrating

	geographical location)
National Center for Children in Poverty http://nccp.org/	Collects data and information and uses research to help form policy and educate the public
National Center of Educational Statistics (Common Core Data—CCD) http://nces.ed.gov/ccd/	Primary database hosting all public K-12 schools in America and the U.S. Territories (contains fiscal and non-fiscal data)
National Center for Health Statistics (Centers for Disease Control—CDC) http://www.cdc.gov/nchs/	Federal government's health vital statistics agency (anything health related)
National Center for Victims of Crime http://www.victimsofcrime.org/library/crime-information-and-statistics	Information related to victims of crime in America
National Forum for Educational Statistics http://nces.ed.gov/forum/	Information and statistics on elementary and secondary education in the United States
National Institute of Literacy http://nces.ed.gov/naal/index.asp	State and county statistics regarding English literacy among American persons aged 16 and older
National Institute of Justice (NIJ)—Geospatial Tools http://www.nij.gov/topics/technology/pages/software-tools.aspx#maps	Free or low cost software tools, apps and databases to assist with criminal/law enforcements, investigations, or research
National Sexual Violence Resource Center http://www.nsvrc.org/organizations/87	Research and information related to sexual violence
National Youth Violence Prevention Resource Center http://www.turningpointmacomb.org/tp/Survivor-Resources/national-youth-violence-prevention-resource-center/	Gateway for professionals, parents, youth, and other interested individuals to gather fact sheets, statistics, and profiles of promising programs
Nation Master http://www.nationmaster.com/	National data for 305 Countries around the globe.
Population Reference Bureau http://www.prb.org/	Informs people around the world about population, health, and the environment and empowers them to use that information to advance the well-being of current and future generations
Public School Review http://www.publicschoolreview.com/	Contains history of public schools, explains the various types, and discusses their pros/cons related to technology on campus, health and nutrition issues, and the latest information related to a variety of student populations
Rural Assistance Center https://www.raconline.org/states/united-states	Socioeconomic statistics, research, and other information about rural

	communities in America
Rural Health (National Institutes of Health) http://www.nlm.nih.gov/hsrinfo/rural_health.html	Information related to rural health outcomes
School Digger http://www.schooldigger.com/	Allows visitors to compare public K-12 schools by test scores, school ranks, school district boundaries, and more
School District Data http://nces.ed.gov/surveys/sdds/index.aspx	Gateway for a number of websites that contain school district data
Small Area Income and Poverty Estimates (SAIPE) http://www.census.gov//did/www/saipe/	Small Area Income and Poverty Estimates (SAIPE) for school districts, counties, and states
Urban Institute http://www.urban.org/	Research, statistics, and policy information related to large U.S. urban areas
Urban and Rural Classification http://www.census.gov/geo/reference/urban-rural.html	Assists visitors in determining whether a particular area has been designated as urban or rural by the U.S. Census
Trading Economics—U.S. Rural Population Data http://www.tradingeconomics.com/united-states/rural-population-percent-of-total-population-wb-data.html	Latest World Bank Indicators values, historical data, forecasts, charts, statistics, economic calendars, and news for rural populations both nationally and globally.

These sites should be able to assist you, or any grant-writer for that matter, with any type of research necessary for grant proposal preparation. My advice is to always use more than one source for grant funding research inquiries because, no matter what any single site says, one single site cannot capture every funding opportunity, no matter how much they try. I also advise you to save these sites in your web browser's "favorites" tab; it will make your search efforts a lot easier.

Final Thoughts

The final thing I will leave with you is that you can't be lazy and *believe* you have the latest information, the most information, or the best information. There will always be new(er) information available. There will always be foundations ceasing operations for various reasons. Federal funding priorities will change with each presidency. Foundations will continue to create new initiatives while shifting away from previous funding priorities/preferences. Additionally, new community foundations will be created every year. Knowing what is available in your local community, state, and nation is vital.

Be alert, be ready, and stay vigilant. Grant funding research is a must. Make it a practice to search weekly for new resources as well as to update your existing resources. This is a great project for interns and anyone being mentored by experienced grant-writers.

Be sure you do your homework and read/reread solicitations, funding opportunity announcements, and grant-maker websites to determine whether or not your organization's priorities and the funders' priorities align. Don't waste your valuable time on resources (grantors) that do not meet the following criteria:

- Is a 100% match with your organization's, project's, or program's needs,
- is focused on funding your particular program or project, or
- is giving within your desired funding range.

Choose your funder(s) wisely, evaluate all aspects of the funding announcement, and (when in doubt) ask.

4. LINKING DATA AND NEEDS TO GRANT FUNDING SOURCES

One of the most difficult things to get nonprofit organizations and governmental entities to understand is the importance of being able to translate your organization's needs to funders. Many organizations have different reasons (and motives) for pursuing funding. Some organizations simply chase dollars. They find the dollars and they apply for the opportunity with no regards for whether they are treading on another charity's territory. Some nonprofits have legitimate needs, but they are unable to provide relative, insightful data illustrating a need and conveying to donors that their organization is worthy of funding. There are some organizations that rely on their own data (whether that one and only source is reliable is always questionable to grant proposal reviewers) because they have no idea how to gather and utilize data resources from other community, state, and national sites to paint a picture of need. If one or more of these scenarios describes your organization, then this section is for you.

In the previous chapter, I provided a number of database resources a nonprofit organization could use for grant proposal development. When using data, it is **IMPERATIVE** that your organization uses the information to tell the entire story. EVERY need you describe in a grant proposal needs to be relative to the solicitation's criteria. While most of the data will be used to demonstrate the needs related to the solicitation, other data will provide context. Be sure you understand the difference as well as the appropriate time to use each type of data. The reason data is so important is because the people that review your proposal may or may not be from your local area or state. Reviewers come from a variety of professional backgrounds, socioeconomic statuses, ages, personal biases (yes, it does exist), and (sometimes) limited understandings of a subject matter due to any number of factors. The most important rule you will need to understand is that each time you write a proposal; you're writing for the audience. The audience will be the review panel or team of peer reviewers charged with deciding whether your application provided enough information to determine whether they can fund it. With that in mind, let me make some helpful tips:

- Reviewers are unable to use outside information to assess whether or not your application is worthy of funding. If you do not provide the information in the application, you have missed an opportunity to share the need.

- Many times, reviewers are unable to consider attachments as relative information, especially in federal applications. Because the application is considered a contract, all of the important information needs to be in black and white within your narrative. Because all federal grant applications are subject to the Freedom of Information Act (FOIA), information in the applications must be written in a manner where any person, regardless of background or geographical location, can determine why the proposal should be funded.

If you do not provide adequate information (data) in the need section, you plainly and simply DO NOT NEED ANY MONEY! Do the homework, find the information, and provide context to **your** problem in order to ensure the person(s) reviewing **your** problem clearly understands. Write clearly and concisely. Sometimes it's not always possible to provide adequate evidence to substantiate organizational, target area, or target population needs—but when it is, be sure to make your evidence of need unmistakably obvious.

Interpreting Criteria: Find the Proper Data to Describe Needs

Now that we have touched on a few important key topics, let's discuss what to use when describing your needs and how to use it. For instance, suppose you're the grant proposal developer for an organization that serves female and adolescent victims of domestic violence in a specific service area. A solicitation may inquire about a number of things to learn about the problem, the proposed community or service area(s) that will benefit from the funding (should the application be awarded), and the specifics regarding the targeted population(s) who will benefit from the funding you are attempting to secure.

Criteria Sample	Suggestions for Responses to Clearly Identify Needs
Describe the service area and target population.	This question/criteria is pretty general/broad. Since the scenario is about female and adolescent domestic violence victims, all of the data should be related to helping a reviewer understand problems in the service area and the populations you plan to serve. Data should describe the following: • the number of people in the county or service area, • the number of criminal domestic violence calls the county receives per year[1] (local data only), • the number of charges, convictions, etc., • poverty rates, demographics, home ownership/rental information, percentage of children/adults/men/women, employment information, geographical distance of county lines for the community AND those of your target population using agency data, • public transportation and basic transportation information, • any cultural information that may assist with context, • age ranges of victims (primary/secondary), • challenges/issues for victims of domestic violence, • victim safety information, • educational attainment data, and • any other data related to describing the criteria.

As you can see, there are a lot of things you may use to describe needs. All the tools you need for collecting this data are listed in the previous chapter. These examples just give you an idea of what you need to provide. Because you are unable to properly address all of the criteria with just your own agency data, you must seek outside sources to address this criteria. Also, don't forget to use multiple sources (and don't forget to cite them, or they aren't legitimate). It's so important to be thorough. Your readers may be unfamiliar with your target area. They can't assume or guess. It must be in black

---

[1] You may also provide comparative data from other nearby surrounding counties or the state for context. Use reliable data (e.g. UCI state law enforcement databases).

Criteria Sample	Suggestions for Responses to Clearly Identify Needs
What problem(s) must be addressed? and white.	This criteria is critical. Even though the criteria is short, it is the one and only opportunity you have to clearly describe the problems related to the reasons why you decided to apply for the grant. - What are the problems YOUR AGENCY discovered that caused you to prepare a grant application? - Only discuss problems tied to the purposes or focus areas of the funder AND your agency. The data you provided in the first section should have been closely connected to this criteria. - If your data do not tie to the solicitation and the problem, find more data. If that is the case, though, it's likely the funding opportunity announcement is not aligned with your project or program mission.

This section is very brief and should be explained clearly and concisely. Unless there are so many problems that a long explanation is required, there is no need to add fluff or drag the problems out. Link the criteria, the solicitation's purpose, and your problem (no exceptions). As a side note, your agency may also decide to provide other published studies and information discovered by your dedicated grant researcher(s) to reinforce your problem while driving home to application reviewers the purpose for your application.

Criteria Sample	Suggestions for Responses to Clearly Identify Needs
Provide a description of current services available within the community to address the needs identified and the gaps in services that currently exist to meet these needs.	In addressing this criteria, you are forced to address a serious question: Is there really a need? Is your organization the only service provider in the community? Is there another provider that provides the same service, but at a higher level? What other services are available related to the purpose of the solicitation and tied to needs, problems, and gaps? In order to address the criteria, you'll need to indicate the following: - the specific names and purposes of organizations in the target area serving the same population with the same needs, - the characteristics of each organization noted (briefly) and any pros or cons as it relates to the beneficiaries from your

	organization, and • all gaps related to the purpose of the solicitation and those your organization discovered via agency needs assessments conducted PRIOR to application preparation.
When preparing this section, it is imperative that the applicant organization knows about ALL service providers in the immediate service area and even those in other counties (or other such areas), as some services are not provided within the immediate targeted area. Pick up the phone, have conversations, review RECENT community needs assessments, and contact law enforcement to see if they can provide your agency with gaps they believe exist. Finally, providing agency data or needs assessments would be helpful and appropriate IN THIS SECTION.	

Criteria Sample	Suggestions for Responses to Clearly Identify Needs
Provide an explanation of how the proposed services and activities will meet the needs that exist.	Again, here is another criteria that is asking the applicant to link the stated needs and gaps with proposed services and activities that will be offered. This criteria may not require as much research homework, as it requires an assessment or inventory of the proposed approach the applicant's organization will prescribe to address the gaps, needs, issues, and problems indicated in the first criteria. Here are some questions to ask: • Does the data illustrate a need and is the prescribed solution tied to it? If not, go back to the drawing board and rethink the need and/or find data to support the need. • Are you suggesting activities/services for which your organization did not provide need data? Is there need data illustrating a problem, but your organization does not provide a solution for the specific problem(s) previously noted? Be sure that everything aligns properly.
This section is pretty self-explanatory. As an application reviewer, I just want to make certain that you comprehend the importance of linking all of the pieces together when attempting to describe needs. All of the pieces to the puzzle need to fit. If not, you will leave reviewers with more questions than answers. If we have to spend a significant amount of time searching for information or reasons for an applicant making a decision to provide services without any data, it's very hard to justify your application to a panel of reviewers. All evidence should leave no doubt as to why your organization's plans are what they are.	

Knowing Where and How to Look Is Half the Battle

Many times I review applications, especially from small or mid-sized organizations, and see that the writer has no clue how to properly describe their needs or problems—the writer doesn't know how to concisely address criteria. It's painful. Sometimes, the persons writing are great at providing services, doing their job, and verbally speaking about the organization when called upon, but they fail miserably when it comes to writing a story that paints a vivid picture. Knowing how to collect data, I believe, is the biggest problem with those applications. A misunderstanding of what is expected by the funder is the main reason these applications fail to be funded. It is such a travesty for an applicant to invest weeks in preparing an application without clearly understanding what is expected by the grant-maker. Do the homework and learn how to comprehend the data and information needed BEFORE attempting to write or prepare the application.

Knowing where to get the information is half the battle. Knowing *where* to place information and *when* to place the information in a grant application in addition to understanding *how* to place the information in the need section of your narrative is just as important as determining eligibility for funding opportunities. If you don't have a need, then you don't need money. If you're unsure whether your work is suitable for submission, ask for help. Have an associate, or someone not affiliated with your employer, but who is familiar with your work (not a close friend—they won't be brutally honest), review your proposal and the scoring rubric or solicitation for clarity and comprehensiveness. Your work should be written at a level where any old Joe from the street could comprehend the problem and the solution handily. Being successful at grant proposal development may mean tossing out some of your old tricks and picking up some new ones. It could mean you get assistance interpreting the solicitation prior to conducting any research. It may also mean that you need to be brutally honest. If your organization doesn't have a strong writer and has been unsuccessful in securing funding, then maybe you need to invest in some training or maybe you need to outsource that aspect of the job for a season until you get some "W's" (wins) under your belt.

Be certain to use the proper data sets to describe your problems or to simplify what is requested in order to provide context for the independent reviewers. If you don't have the time to conduct thorough research, you shouldn't attempt to write. There are no ifs, ands, or buts about it. Take time to start looking at various private and public funding solicitations to practice interpreting criteria and conducting research. The only way to learn how to do it properly is to practice. At the end of this book, I'll provide a site where interested writers can send sample narratives written by individuals in order to provide reviews. Great research makes perfect proposals. No one starts out perfect, but we all can finish the race perfectly. I'll conduct one more scenario which will (hopefully) help you better understand the importance of research (no matter the subject matter, target area, target population, or purpose), the thought processes that need to happen prior to conducting the research (the type of information needed to respond to solicitation criteria), the best places to find data, and the process of collecting it.

The next scenario will be for a governmental entity seeking to address community policing in light of all the issues associated with accountability and transparency. A police department or city agency is seeking funding for body cameras from a federal grant funder. Using the scenarios in the media (without any personal bias and preferences of course), pretend you are writing this application on behalf of a mid-size or large police department or sheriff department in a large city that has been in the news due to high profile shootings of unarmed persons, a mistrust of law-enforcement, and any protests, marches, or riots following the shooting.

Simple Grant Research Funding- Chapter 4

Criteria Sample	Suggestions for Responses to Clearly Identify Needs
Provide evidence in support of your organization's need for body-cameras (BCs).	Because this scenario is specifically related to law enforcement/criminal justice, violent crimes, deaths, lawsuits, etc., data will be VERY specific and will likely come from the law enforcement agency seeking this type of funding opportunity. Evidence may include the following: • The number of incidents where injury or death has occurred between civilians and law enforcement during a specific (and recent) period of time (no less than seven years, unless you are able to tie certain specific changes with increases and decreases for a different time span), • the total number of lawsuits the city/county/municipality/law enforcement agency has settled, • the actual dollar amount of all total cases settled within the specified time frame used to describe evidence of issues, • the total number of complaints and civil disputes with descriptions of the types of incidents, • the evidence of public trust issues (cite news sources, community surveys, etc.), and/or • any other relative information that may be used to describe the need for body cameras.

Criteria Sample	Suggestions for Responses to Clearly Identify Needs
Describe the demographics of your authority/jurisdiction.	When addressing this criteria, you would provide a wide array of demographic information that is tied to the need for body cameras. • Describe the areas (e.g. zip codes, streets, subdivisions, apartment complexes) in which patrolmen will utilize the body cameras. These areas could be described by age ranges, income information (average/median), educational attainment rate information, arrest information (recent), crime data (recent), child protective services information,

	employment trend information, homeownership information, total population, crime watch community data, death rates (via law enforcement), etc. Some information may come from law enforcement while other information will come from other databases in the previous chapter. Please don't make the mistake of using only one source (law enforcement data) to describe the target need. Other information from outside sources, such as Uniform Crime Reporting (UCR), Census Bureau, or American Community Survey data, provides additional context for grant reviewers regarding the potential issues in your targeted jurisdiction (s).

Criteria Sample	Suggestions for Responses to Clearly Identify Needs
Demonstrate a full understanding of how officer complaints and use-of-force practices can be addressed by BCs.	In attempting to address this criteria, instead of providing data (which can't be used to answer this criteria), you will need to provide STRONG, evidence-based research to substantiate an understanding of how complaints can be decreased or eliminated with the use of body cameras. This evidence needs to directly correlate to the target populations and issues you cited in the criteria above to help guide evaluations by reviewers of your agency's need. You will also likely want to address issues by advocacy groups and civil liberties agencies to describe how your need for BCs will help decrease/address concerns by such groups.

Final Thoughts

I'd like to clarify one thing. Being a governmental agency with years and years of experience doesn't mean you'll get a free pass to skimp on information needed to assess your application appropriately. As a reviewer, I have a higher expectation of governmental agencies than I do community-based organizations because governmental agencies have access to more resources and some of the best data collection tools available as well as legislation, which often requires those agencies to collaborate cohesively. In my mind, this means there are no excuses. I'm often disappointed when I see a poorly written application from a large state or governmental entity because they often have the most information at their fingertips to make a case for support. Misinterpreting criteria and not investing in the development of writers will be your down falls.

Whether you're writing for a small police department or a state agency, such as Children/Family Services or Bureau of Investigation, you MUST do the same amount of work in telling your stories.

There is no free pass, as reviewers use the same criteria writers use in preparing their grant proposals and narratives. Please don't skimp. Don't believe that reviewers will assume, because they aren't allowed to. Do your due diligence and find the appropriate data and evidence to substantiate your request. I hope these scenarios will help writers understand the criteria a little better. Write as if you're the funder or reviewer, not a person passionate about your agency, your work, and/or your mission.

Changing your mindset helps you paint a better picture—tell a better story to the readers. Practice comprehending the criteria. Without proper comprehension of the criteria, it's impossible to provide accurate data and evidence. If you're ever in doubt about what some aspects of the criteria mean, ask others in your office to ensure that your line of thinking is correct. To confirm, contact the program officer to receive clarification on what the criteria means. There is nothing wrong with asking questions. There *is* something wrong with not inquiring when you're uncertain about some aspects of criteria and, instead, submitting a narrative that's way off course, rambling about data irrelevant to the solicitation/problem for applications because a writer "thought" they were on track. Ask questions **EARLY** in the proposal preparation process, research **DILIGENTLY,** and learn to write **CONCISELY**.

5. PROGRAM PLANNING AND BUDGET DEVELOPMENT

When developing programs and budgets, the preparation of the two sections must go hand in hand with the problem, need, and the solicitation criteria. It's quite easy to develop a proposal for an existing program with an existing budget. It's very difficult, however, to develop a proposal and budget for a new program, project, problem, or need within an organization. This section is primarily for the one-stop shop grant-writer, but the information may also benefit individuals that work on teams and don't often have a chance to prepare a program or budget for a grant proposal. In order to understand how valuable the portion of the proposal you develop is, I believe you must understand the full proposal development process.

Budget Planning Relevancy

I bet you're wondering "how does program planning and budget development and research connect?" In order to prepare a reasonable and feasible budget, you need to conduct research on salaries and wages to ensure they are fair, reasonable, and within the range of other wages offered in the targeted and surrounding areas. Grant-writers and researchers need to find the most accurate and recent fringe benefit calculations[1] (when applicable). The same applies for equipment and supply expenses. If planning to hire consultants, the writer must get quotes from several and attempt to assess the total amount needed to compensate these individuals offering specialized services. Writers must calculate overhead expenses, and many other types of ordinary and out of the ordinary expenses. Knowing where to go and how to research such expenses are keys to preparing a successful budget in a timely manner, especially for new programs/projects.

When reviewers (including myself) assess your budgets, we must take into consideration your entire proposal first and foremost. Reviewers (we) look to make sure your proposal directly correlates to the proposed budget and to ensure your requests are responsive to the needs noted in the problem/need statement. Secondly, we go through **EACH** and **EVERY** budget category in order to assess whether there are any outrageous requests (yes, some agencies attempt to fleece us). Finally, we read budget narratives to determine whether the reasons for requests are aligned with the purpose of the solicitation as well as your request. Please know that there are some budget hawks on every review panel; I am one of them. With a background in business administration (nonprofit) and familiarity with nonprofit mismanagement and budget appropriations, I take a thorough approach to looking over proposal budgets. A lot of old rules need to be tossed out of the window when it comes to grant-writing, like asking for an unnecessary (and expensive) computer with every grant application.

Allow me to provide you with some basic guidance on conducting budget research. The table below notes places most commonly used to find costs related to program budgets. Please keep in mind that there are a number of places that writers may use which are specialized based on the nature of business (e.g. higher education, law enforcement, K-12 education, social/human services). Regardless of the category, please be mindful that the dollars you are seeking are neither free nor unlimited. Make sure your requests are reasonable and necessary. Budgets often illustrate an applicant's true intentions and may cause a panel to reconsider an application's worthiness due to frivolous and outrageous requests. Also, as it relates to salaries, it is important to do your homework. Nonprofits have this idea that they

---

[1] Fringe Benefits are benefits provided by an employer to an employee, independent contractor, or partner. Benefits include Social Security taxes, Medicare, Federal unemployment, health insurance, group-term life insurance coverage, educational assistance, childcare and assistance reimbursement, cafeteria plans, employee discounts, employee stock options, personal use of a company-owned vehicle, and others.

must be "thrifty" by skimping on employee compensation and forgoing the opportunity to hire the "best" talent for the "*cheapest*" talent. Allow your projects, programs, and services to have the best (period).

Budget Item/ Category	Reason for Researching	Where to Find Information
Salaries	Your agency should make sure salaries are in line with salaries that other agencies in the area are offering to staff for the same position title (excluding special circumstances where staff may possess a higher level of experience, special certifications, etc.). With all the fuss today about fair living wages, you don't want to be on the wrong side of history or perceived as cheap.	Your state employment agency is the best place to search for the most accurate rates. After that, try the following: Salary.com Payscale.com Professionals for Nonprofits Salary Survey Indeed.com Simply Hired U.S. Bureau of Labor Statistics—U.S. Department of Labor
Fringe Benefits	Fringe benefits are the extra perks of the job: vacation pay, retirement, medical, dental and vision insurance, premiums, training and tuition reimbursement, life insurance contributions, long-term disability plans, and other company-paid perks.	Most of your research will come from your agency's human resources and/or payroll department. Be sure to the calculate cost of living increases where applicable and the expected annual increases for health insurance premiums, etc. For salary/fringe benefits calculations, visit the Pay Check City Website: http://www.paycheckcity.com/calculator/salary/
Office Supplies	Office supply costs may vary. Some agency's shop locally (e.g. grocery stores, local office supply stores). Whenever possible, research any/all amounts used to come up with an accurate supply budget. It ensures you expend all of your funds and there are no questions with round numbers.	You can use a variety of methods to calculate office expense. Use a legitimate number to calculate your cost at all times. Reviewers shop for office supplies too; they know that rarely, if ever, do you find a price with a rounded number. Use the following aids in office supply budget calculations: Quill.com Office Supply.com Staples.com Office Max.com
Educational Supplies	Break downs for these types of expenses in budget justifications are	Because some things like curriculum supplies and supplemental materials must be purchased directly from the developer, it's not reasonable

	really important because they give reviewers a general idea of your plans so they can determine whether the purchases are approach-related.	to list such resources. Here are a few great, basic resources for supplies to be used for K-12 educational programs: Discount School Supply.com K-12 School Supplies.net School Outfitters
Office Equipment and Furniture	A good justification for office furniture and equipment is required. Please let me advise you not to get the most expensive, top of the line items because you WANT them, as opposed to NEED them. While reviewers and funders do understand some organizations may need more expensive, high quality items (e.g. health care providers, schools, public agencies dealing with sensitive issues), most organizations can generally can get by with "regular" stuff. If you don't need it, don't ask for it. Many other organizations are fighting for the same dollars and many that have to do more with less because more established organizations tend to be hogs, eating up all the funds from other baby agencies seeking to get a piece of the pie. I know many will disagree with me, but in a time where we are recovering from a recession, along with the large number of persons seeking public services these days, funders and reviewers are taking a	Some organizations may use local, small business suppliers. Before purchasing new furniture, I would check with your state to see if there is surplus that can be purchased at little or no cost to nonprofits. State agencies, school districts, police departments, etc. purchase furniture and equipment with taxpayer dollars. When upgrading, they place those older, gently used items in a warehouse to collect dust. Some states sell all items to anyone interested in purchasing them and some states donate items to charities with proof of tax-exempt status. For those in need of figures for office equipment and furniture, here are some great sites to search for information: Best Buy.com Office Max.com Office Depot.com Staples.com Grainger.com E-Office Direct.com Modern Office My Chef Store (industrial kitchen) Food Service Warehouse (industrial kitchen) CKitchen.com (industrial kitchen) Apple.com Hewlett Packard.com Dell.com Microsoft.com Lenovo.com Acer.com Asus.com

	look at organizations as a whole as well as their programmatic and organizational budgets when considering grant awards. Ask wisely.	

Final Thoughts

I hope this information will provide some guidance for budget preparation. These are basic items that I've seen over the years where grant proposals tend to overshoot or undershoot. Budget scores are not usually assigned a lot of points, but a poorly prepared budget could cause you to miss a few points and miss the funding threshold cut off during the application scoring process. Spend quality time conducting research for the items for which you are seeking outside funding. Be prepared to justify and fight for what it is that you are requesting. If it's not worth fighting for and you can't justify it, you likely don't need it. So, don't include it in your budget. It's not simply about being frugal; it's about being honest and operating with integrity. Questionable items in a budget may cause reviewers to question the integrity of the applicant. Research and prepare with integrity.

6. FINDING AND INTERPRETING PRIVATE FOUNDATION—990 TAX RETURNS

This may be one of the most complicated chapters in this book to understand. However, learning how to read and interpret 990-Forms will assist you in understanding giving trends of private funders, operational trends of nonprofit organizations (while discovering who potential target area the competitors are), the organization's funded during a fiscal year, and the assets available for the grants. Public agencies, such as law enforcement agencies, public schools, colleges and universities, and local governments, are funded primarily by city, county, and state funds. Those agencies do not use 990-Forms because of the organizations' business-designated operations status as a state or governmental agency. Because of the Freedom of Information Act, most (if not all) states have budget information for every agency receiving state funding on a state budget website. I will provide that information later in this chapter for each state.

The IRS Form 990

The IRS Form 990 is an annual tax return reporting form that certain, federally tax-exempt organizations MUST file with the IRS. The form contains valuable information, such as the filing organization's mission, programs, finances (revenue and expenses), and funds dispersed in the form of grants or fellowships. Private foundations must use this form, making it an excellent tool for researching potential funding sources. This form must be filed every year by organizations with gross receipts greater than or equal to $200,000 or total assets greater than or equal to $500,000. Federally tax-exempt organizations with gross receipts of less than $200,000 or total assets of less than $500,000 may file a 990-EZ, which is a shorter version of the 990. Both forms can be found online and are free to access and review in a number of places: GuideStar, the Foundation Center, Charity Navigator, the Economic Research Institute, etc.

Why Is the Form Important

You can find useful tidbits in these returns, such as the examples listed here:

- who sits on the board of directors,
- the mission of the organization and the grant applicant process,
- the amount of assets the tax-exempt organization possesses,
- compensation information,
- the name, address, and type of grantees awarded grants within a specific fiscal/tax year,
- any other types of long-term financial commitments made to charities, colleges, universities, or nonprofit organizations,
- grant award sizes and ranges during a fiscal/tax year,
- addresses, phone numbers, and names of program staff or contact persons,
- web addresses,
- grant-maker preferences, and/or
- any changes in mission or giving guidelines.

I have provided two links to sample 990 return forms that will assist you in gaining some understanding on how to extract information from returns. I recommend printing the forms in order to view the returns comprehensively. I also advise you to practice reviewing these forms online in order to become acclimated with the different appearances of each return. Because organizations have different asset amounts and varying grant-making guidelines that may impact the number of awards made throughout a fiscal year, some returns may have more pages than others. I have reviewed some returns that have more than 200 pages and other returns with as few as 47 pages. Therefore, practicing and learning how to hunt for the information needed to make informed decisions regarding whether to apply to certain private grant-making organizations will save you valuable time conducting the actual research when the time comes.

Sample 990-EZ Returns
www.sweetadelineintl.org/.../files/Form 990

990 PF (Private Foundation) Return (Whole Planet Foundation)
https://www.wholeplanetfoundation.org/about/financials/

Use the resources in previous chapters of this book to practice searching the private foundations you come in contact with. The information will be a vital aspect of the research process. Practice makes perfect and you will need to develop a comfort level and passion for searching for the best matches for your organization.

Which Schedules Are Important and Why

Typically, I search for certain schedules (forms) within a private foundation's 990 returns. This information helps me get right to the point, skipping all of the other "important," yet irrelevant, information for the purposes of our research efforts. Browse other schedules if you like, but remember that some information you may be searching for is time sensitive.

1. **Schedule A (Public Charity Status and Public Support)**
   This schedule (form) provides information about a private foundation's present operating status and public support. It also provides helpful information like the foundation's mission statement or other descriptions of its benevolent/charitable goals.
2. **Schedule B (Schedule of Contributors)**
   This schedule is used to demonstrate contributions made to the organization reported on Form 990. Sometimes, smaller community foundations secure grant funding from larger foundations to disseminate at the community level. Always know how to connect the dots to follow the money trails.
3. **Schedule D (Supplemental Financial Statements)**
   This schedule is used by private foundations (as well as other nonprofits) to simply provide additional financial information. A brief scan is in accordance. You never know what relevant information you may find.
4. **Schedule I (Grants and Other Assistance to Organizations, Governments, and Individuals In The United States)**
   This schedule is used by private foundations (and other organizations) to describe grants and other assistance made by a private foundation during the tax year to domestic (U.S.) organizations, domestic governments, and domestic individuals (in the form of fellowships and scholarships).
5. **Schedule J (Compensation Information)**
   This schedule is used by private foundations to disclose the compensation information for certain officers, directors, individual trustees, key employees, and highest compensated employees as well as other information related to the foundation's compensation practices

within the organization. This information is helpful in determining who makes funding decisions and how much time each person dedicates to the organization weekly, quarterly, and/or annually. This schedule provides insight as to who is involved with day to day operations and whether the foundation's directors spend much time working on behalf of the mission.

6. **Schedule L (Transactions With Interested Persons)**
   This schedule is used by private foundations to detail the financial assistance benefiting interested persons. This assistance could be in the form of scholarships, internships, prizes, awards, use of facilities, etc., awarded to any qualified person(s) or major potential donors. This information is helpful to researchers seeking private foundations making educational grants and scholarships to individuals. This will likely be the schedule where you will find grant awards and long-term commitment distributions made to grantees during a specific financial period. Be sure to look for these important tidbits of information:

   - grant ranges (i.e. smallest to largest award made) and their relations to each other,
   - type of organization (e.g. social/human service organization, schools, fire houses, colleges, hospitals, animal shelters, religious institutions, national organizations, community foundations),
   - any organization(s) that receive multiple grants awards within a single tax year,
   - funding/giving/award preferences (e.g. colleges vs. social services or education vs. healthcare), and/or
   - locations of grantee organizations (e.g. regionally, nationally, within the state of the private foundation).

7. **Schedule O (Supplemental Information to Form 990 Or 990-EZ)**
   This schedule is very important. Private foundations use this form to place excess information that was unable to fit on any particular schedule. In this section, researchers will find grantee information regarding the charities that received grants from a specific private foundation during a funding cycle/grant year. This section can have unlimited pages, so please take your time and go through it carefully.

Take Away

While this may appear as a lot of schedules to review in order to determine whether a private foundation is a perfect fit for your organization, it is the *"preferred"* method of many grant prospectors (researchers). Utilizing these schedules have helped me assess whether a private grant-making foundation's website matches up with their charter and mission. Sometimes, their website and charters state one thing, but giving patterns may reflect something totally contrary. This is one of the frustrating things about submitting blind proposals, in my opinion. Therefore, scrutinizing PF-990s has proven to be a helpful screening tool for me in my private grant-maker profile research efforts. Discovering discrepancies or conflicts between mission and giving practices early is a great way to avoid wasting time preparing applications. It has also helped to avoid sending potential clients on wild goose chases that will likely yield absolutely nothing. Reviewing the information in the schedules, as I have described, is an experience that develops essential core research skills that are valuable for new grant prospectors to master. Explaining why your rates are what they are and what your work entails is helpful for business billing and quote purposes.

Final Thoughts

This is a pretty intense chapter. If you hate taxes, you likely hate this chapter. I encourage you to become more familiar with scanning through these forms. It's a fantastic treasure for grant-seekers. When in doubt about any information found within a private foundation's PF-990, please pick up the phone and call the grant-maker to discuss your findings, especially where conflicts exist between website information and actual giving/grant-making practices.

Please be aware that it is possible that the fiscal years you find during your searches *"may"* run a year or two behind current years. Therefore, you will need to understand that information is not "current," but reflects prior grant-making trends of previous years. Please use the resources below in order to find PF-990 data.

Website	Web Address
Charity Navigator	www.charitynavigator.org
Guide Star	guidestar.org
Foundation Center	foundationcenter.org
Serious Givers	seriousgivers.org/be-a-data-shepherd/find-charity-990/
IRS	www.irs.gov/Charities-%26-Non-Profits/Form-990-Resources-and-Tools-for-Researchers
National Center for Charitable Statistics	http://www.nccs.urban.org/
Economic Research Institute	http://www.eri-nonprofit salaries.com/index.cfm?FuseAction=NPO.Search

7. GRANT FUNDER AND GRANT-WRITING TERMS

If you are a veteran grant-writer and/or grant researcher, this chapter may be a refresher course. If you are new to grant research and comprehending application criteria, funding opportunity announcements, and/or solicitations for grant funding, then you will soon learn many terms that are used within the realm of grant research that will be new territory to you. The nonprofit sector in general has their own terms—their own language when it comes to describing different elements and aspects of grant-writing. In order to understand what the funder desires, grant researchers must understand the terms used. Comprehension is the key to preparing a successful grant proposal. I have compiled a list of terms and put my own spin on them to provide novices with some additional guidance in a manner to which they can relate.

There are so many different terms for so many different focus areas that it is nearly impossible to capture them all. At the end of the terminology section, you will find additional resources that may help you understand the terms used in funding opportunity announcements. When in doubt, call the funder and ask (be sure to get names and remember dates). Never assume you understand the meaning of the terms. It is always better to not know and ask rather than to not know and assume. Providing the wrong information in your grant proposal because of your misunderstanding of one term in one criteria could be the determinant of whether or not you make the funding threshold cut.

Grant-writing Terms

Absolute Priority: any condition that must be met before a grant application will be considered for funding; most often associated with federal funding.

Abstract (also called Executive Summary): a one-page, typed summary of a grant proposal or narrative; briefly describes the purpose for the application.

Activities: the specific events, actions, or services to be conducted in order to achieve the goals and objectives of the program or project indicated in a grant proposal or narrative.

Administrative Costs (also called Administrative Expenses and Operating Costs): costs not directly associated with or connected to the operation of an organization, project, or program; can negatively or positively impact the financial well-being and strength of an organization. (Examples include rent, utilities, administrative staff [Directors and Administrative Assistants], and insurance.)

Advance Payment (also called Start-up Funding): monies requested by the grant applicant; often requested within a grant application and requested prior to being awarded. (Advance payment options are not always available to grantees.)

Agency: (1) the organization providing services or pursuing grant funding. (2) the agency seeking applicants to which to award grants.

Allowable Activities or Costs: activities or costs associated with a current or proposed project or program that are allowed by the funder; usually noted prior to the closing of the application deadline. (Applications with unallowable activities and costs are usually down-scored or rejected for funding. With high scoring applications [fundable], applicants are typically asked by the funder to rework budgets prior to being "officially" awarded.)

Annual Performance Report: a report sought by the funder describing the grant applicant's activities, outcomes, accomplishments, problems, and other metrics illustrating progress towards stated goals and objectives.

Application: the formal process and document used to pursue grant funding; can consist of a combination of formal funding agency forms or a simple narrative with suggested subheadings and categories encouraged by the funder.

Application for Federal Assistance (also called the SF (Standard Form)—424): the official/standard form for federal grant funding assistance.

Application Package: all forms required in order to submit a formal request related to a specific funding opportunity announcement.

Appropriations Legislation: a federal, state, or local law passed to provide certain levels of funding for a grant program for a specified or an unspecified period of time.

Asset-Based Initiatives: an initiative that is developed based on the strengths and resources of the individuals and the organization that add additional resources (human, financial, etc.) to a grant program or project, allowing it to be more efficient and/or to operate at a higher capacity.

Asset-Based Mapping: the process of a group or community coming together to assess (make an inventory of) local or regional assets; documented in visual aid form to illustrate community resources for community and grant development.

Assets: individual, organizational, and/or communal skills, talents, gifts, or resources (human, financial, natural, in-kind, etc.) shared with a community or organization; listed within a grant application.

Audit (financial): a thorough, independent evaluation of an organization's financial documents, policies, procedures, and programs to render an opinion of fairness, consistency, and conformity within generally accepted practices and principles; primarily conducted at the end of a fiscal (financial) year. (Some grants may require an audit at the end of a grant cycle or grant period.)

Audit (programmatic) (also called Program Monitoring): a review of the accomplishments of grant-funded programs by funding agency staff, consultants, or external evaluators; can be organized and structured or completely random.

Authorized Organizational Representative (AOR): the person(s) responsible for submitting and/or signing grant applications; attests with his/her signature that all assurances and certifications are true

Authorizing Legislation: a law passed by Congress or state legislation which establishes/permits and furthers continuation of a grant program; primarily used with public (federal and state) grant funding awards.
.

Award: a formal electronic or snail mail notice (which sometimes includes a check) officially presenting a grant gift to an applicant organization; may also include other agreements and contracts that must be completed prior to starting and continuing the program or project for which the applicant organization was awarded.

Awarding Agency: the organization or funder officially offering and/or administering the grant award; term primarily used with public (federal and state) grant funding awards.

Beneficiary: persons within the targeted area or population who will benefit from programs and services made possible by a grant award.

Block Grant: grants from formula funds[1] not allocated to specific categories or legislation; flexible in regards to the manner and method of distribution.

Boilerplate: a template or master grant narrative created by grant-writers that uses common grant proposal components and headings; often used to mass produce various types of grant proposals, primarily by new nonprofits. (A boilerplate should only be used as a one-stop shop for information—not as a copy and paste method for completing grant applications.)

Brick and Mortar: capital (investment) grants used for building or renovating buildings and/or construction projects.

Budget: the total costs of operating a program, project, or organization. (Funders may seek various types of budgets from grant applicants [e.g. Program/Project Budget, Operating Budget, Annual Budget].)

Capacity: an organization's or collaborative group's ability to share resources (human, financial, physical) for the purposes of program or community building and/or grant implementation.

Capacity Building Grants: grants for public and nonprofit organizations that assist in enhancing organizational capacity as well as other important issues of organizational development and effectiveness. (Areas of capacity building often include strategic planning/re-tooling, organizational development/assessments, board development, technical assistance, funding for new staff positions, executive transitions, social enterprise, funds development, strategic restructuring, and more.)

Catalog Federal Domestic Assistance (CFDA) Number: identifies a specific federal assistance program. (The first two numbers help identify the specific federal agency for each legislatively authorized program. For example, the prefix "93" is designated for grants awarded by the U.S. Department of Health and Human Services.)

Challenge Grant: used to stimulate additional fundraising by awarding grant funding only if the grant applicant raises funds from other resources. (A written commitment [as proof] is often required before awards are made.)

Closeout: the process of tying up the loose ends as an agency winds down at the end of a grant funding cycle. (Grant-makers sometimes have processes and forms that an organization must complete prior to ending all work related to a grant award.)

Community Based Organization (CBO): a private, nonprofit organization that provides services or offers projects within a specific community.

---

[1] Formula grants are funding programs that agencies do not compete for. They are given to designated recipients and are usually administered and managed by State Administering Agencies.

Community Development Block Grant (CDBG): grant funds used to develop public and private entities that aid in a community's development priorities for low-income communities. (CDBG projects benefit low-income persons, prevent/eliminate blight, and/or aid other serious community development needs. The program is administered by the U.S. Department of Health and Human Services [HUD].)

Community Foundation: an organization supported publicly that awards grants within a specific county, region, or community; receive funds from donors and write grants to larger foundations that support the works of smaller community foundations. (Community foundations may have a variety of focus areas to which they award, but focus areas are primarily based on community needs.)

Company Foundation (also called Corporate Foundation): a private foundation funded and established by a private, for-profit business for charitable purposes. (Examples include Walmart, Coca Cola, McDonalds, Purina, Mac, Johnson & Johnson, Budweiser, Target, Macy's)

Competition ID: the number assigned to a funding opportunity announcement by the grant-making/awarding agency.

Competitive Grant: a grant process during which the grant-making agency rates and ranks eligible applications prior to making awards. (Applications with the highest scores receive grant awards.)

Competitive Review Process (also called Peer Review or Grant Review): the process of selecting applications for grant awards; conducted by a panel of subject matter experts. (Applications are read, discussed, and scored by subject matter (or subject area) by expert panelists using the rating criteria (usually directly from the funding announcement) provided by the grant-making agency.)

Continuation Grant: a new grant award for a project previously funded by the same funding agency.

Contract: a grant award of sub-award and/or a procurement[2] sub-contract under a recipients or sub-recipient's contract.

Corporate Giving Program: a grant-making program funded and administered by a for-profit business such as Comcast, Bank of America, and Microsoft.

Data Universal Numbering System (DUNS): a unique, nine-character identification number provided by the commercial company Dun & Bradstreet (D&B) free of charge. (Every applicant applying for a federal grant must have a DUNS number prior to submitting an application.)

Deadline: the due date for a grant proposal submission/acceptance. (All funders will clearly specify application deadlines within funding opportunity announcements.)

Demonstration Project: a grant project used to demonstrate new methods or services within a specific focus area. (There is usually a call for demonstration projects by a grant-maker prior to an application being submitted.)

---

[2] A competition offering fair access to prospective bidders that directs how purchases are made

Direct Costs: costs directly connected to operating a grant (or organizational) program; designated as such for the sole purpose of being reimbursed by a grant funding agency. (Direct costs may include direct service program staff, consultants, supplies, travel, and/or equipment.)

Disallowed Costs (also called Unallowed Costs): costs identified by a grant funder that are noted as impermissible or unallowable in accordance with federal and grant funder cost principles; usually noted prior to the grant application submission process in the funding opportunity announcement.

Discretionary Grants: grants awarded based on determinations made by the funding agency. (Grant funding is usually limited and awarded based on the funders predetermined preferences.)

Dissemination of Information: the process of sharing information related to the outcome(s) or existence of the grant program/project. (Funders often want organizations to tell the world about its works as well as how their funds were used to help/improve the community. Information to be shared can include (but is not limited to) program/project activities, evaluation results, and closeout activities.)

Diversity: the differences within a community or organization (race, ethnicity, age, economic status, income, talent pool, educational background, family composition, sexual orientation, religion, etc.); the awareness and acknowledgement of all the different aspects of a particular community. (Many federal funders inquire about and are interested in diversity.)

Draw Down: the act of a grantee or grant applicant requesting funds (payments) throughout the project period; requested electronically via electronic funds transfer (EFT) or via mail with supportive documentation validating payment is due. (Funds may be drawn down prior to start the grant award, weekly, monthly, or other designated times.)

E-Application: a grant application that is submitted online. (Sometimes, grant-makers provide templates for online submissions. Other times, the criteria is provided and applicants can create their own formats and templates for submission. Review the grant-maker's guidelines carefully when submitting E-Applications, as additional supporting documentation may be required.)

ED: The U.S. Department of Education.

Education Department General Administrative Regulations (EDGAR): policies developed by the Grants Policy and Oversight Staff for discretionary grantee guidance on program and project implementation.

Eligible Activities: activities that are approved by the funder for a particular grant program. (Be sure to find out what each funder allows prior to preparing your grant application. When in doubt, *always* ask.)

Eligible Applicants: applicants, entities, or nonprofit organizations deemed eligible to apply for grant funding from a specific funder.

Endowment Funds: a large amount of money set aside in support of a school, hospital, etc.; used to pay for the creation and continuation of long-term support.

English as Second Language (ESL): describes programs serving immigrants whose first language is not English.

Expenses: expenditures and costs associated with doing business or, in the case of nonprofits, the actual costs associated with operating.

Family Foundation: an independent, tax-exempt, private foundation where the primary source of funding comes from members of one family.

Federal Register (FR): a daily digest for rules, proposed rules, and notices of the United States Government produced via the Office of the Federal Register, the National Archives and Records Administration, and the U.S. Government Printing Office. (Funding Opportunity Announcements will fall under the Notices section. Interested individuals can subscribe to specific notices and alerts via email online at the Federal Register website free of charge as a service to the public.)

Federated Giving Programs (also called the Middle-man): a joint fundraising initiative usually administered by a nonprofit umbrella (e.g. United Way or Red Cross). (Many employers run fundraising campaigns on behalf of such organizations annually in order to support programs that are awarded grants via the federated giving program.)

Fiscal Year: a business's or nonprofit organization's 12-month accounting period. (During this time, agency books are closed and reconciled and annual reports and audits are conducted in order to account for organizational finances [revenues and expenses].)

Form 990-PF: the IRS tax form used by all private foundations (nonprofits) which demonstrates to the general public a record of financial transactions (revenues and expenses) as well as fundraising and grant information.

Formula Grant: a noncompetitive, state grant award based on a predetermined formula set by Congress. Formula grant programs are also called state-administered programs, funded by the federal government.

Full-time equivalent (FTE): accounting term used to describe a financial obligation for a full-time employee; mostly used in budgets and budget justifications.

Funder (also called grant-maker or grantor): the entity or organization distributing grant funds.

Funding Agency (also called grantor): agency making grant awards.

Funding Cycle: a grant-maker's timetable or calendar of events which includes any informational sessions or webinars, the release of the funding opportunity announcement (request for proposals [RFPs]), application submission, application review, award offer period, official award notification, and release of grant award funds.

Funding Offer: the official notification or offer made by the funder; made via snail mail, email, or official contracts sent express mail. (Sometimes, offers and awards are made first verbally, but they are not "official" until an offer is made in writing on the grant-making agency's official letter head.)

Funding Opportunity Announcement (FOA): a notice on Grants.gov of a federal grant opportunity.

Funding Priorities or Funding Preferences: objective factors used to award extra rating points during the grant review process to grant applicants who meet the pre-established criteria. (Competitions with funding preferences and priorities are primarily used during the federal grant competition, but some state grant awards also include funding priorities and preferences.)

General Operating Support: grants awarded to support day to day operations of a nonprofit organization; does not have to be program or project specific; used to pay overhead costs, administrative expenses, staff salaries, repair costs, etc.; generally viewed as a "thumbs up" for doing great work.

Grant: a source of money awarded to an organization (and, sometimes, to individuals) in order to perform specific activities; sometimes serve as contracts to perform services in exchange for grant funding.

Grant Agreement: formal agreements (contracts) between a grantee and a grantor.

Grantee: the organization or entity awarded/receiving a grant award; responsible for carrying out all dissemination, administration, and reporting responsibilities. (In the event there is a joint application or collaboration grant, only one entity may be the grantee.)

Grantor: the state entity, corporate foundation, federal agency, or private grant-making foundation making grant awards.

Grassroots: a group or organization that is created and run by persons (usually locally) with or without persons with professional experience affiliated.

Guidelines: the specific grantor instructions used to prepare a grant application.

HHS: The U.S. Department of Health and Human Services.

HUD: The U.S. Department of Housing and Urban Development.

Indirect Cost Rate: the rate (or percentage) of an organization's indirect costs to its direct costs; a formal method of charging individual programs for their share of indirect costs; used in the award of federal (and state) contracts, grants, and other assistance arrangements governed by the federal government.

Indirect Costs: costs that are not easily identifiable or directly associated with operating a grant program or project (including overhead costs, administration, building maintenance, insurance, etc.).

In-Kind Contribution: a non-cash contribution of labor (volunteer or professional services, accommodations/amenities, services, equipment, food, supplies, etc.) that can be used as matching funds; can be valued at a rate; often valued at a much higher per dollar an hour rate than minimum wage.

Invitational Priorities: a special invitation by grant-makers to apply for grants with a preference given to applicants that address specific grantor priorities and/or preferences.

IRS: Internal Revenue Service.

Lead Agency (Applicant): the grantee (of a collaboration) responsible for implementing and overseeing grant program activities in a collaborative or joint grant application.

Lead Agency (Funder): the grant-making agency responsible for approving, overseeing, and evaluating grant activities.

Lead Education Agency (LEA): a term used when referencing state educational agencies, schools, and districts by the federal and state governments.

Letter of Commitment: a formal letter addressed to the grant-making agency declaring what specific services or other contributions (in-kind, fee-for-service, etc.) will be contributed to a proposed project. (In many cases, such letters are requested by the grant-making agency. Letters are signed and dated and they reference the specific funding opportunity for which resources are to be committed.)

Letter of Intent: a letter from a prospective applicant indicating interest in applying for a grant prior to the grant submission deadline; usually required by the grant-making agency. (Submission guidelines are almost always provided.)

Letter of Support: a letter from partner organizations, community leaders, and other stakeholders submitted in conjunction with a grant application illustrating support for the proposed application or program; usually requested by the grant-making agency; must reference the specific funding opportunity.

Leveraging Ratio: see Matching Grants.

Mandatory Grants: see Formula Grants.

Match: see Matching Grant.

Matching Grant (also called Challenge Grants): a grant awarded for the purpose of matching funds awarded or promised by another donor or grant-making entity.

Memorandum of Agreement (MOA): a formal agreement between two or more entities illustrating the purpose for which the entities came together, a brief (but relative) description of each entity, contributions (financial, services, or in-kind) each entity will make to the proposed collaboration, names of persons assisting in decision making and preparing the MOU, a reference to the specific funding opportunity announcement, current signatures and dates, and other components as required by the grant-making agency.

Memorandum of Understanding (MOU): see Memorandum of Agreement.

Monitoring (see Audit for additional information): the overseeing of activities conducted by the grantee, the grantor, and (at times) the independent evaluators.

Needs Assessment: an evaluation or inventory of needs within a community, organization, or subject area which enables the applicant to justify a grant request or substantiate the need for new programs and/or services.

Non-Competitive Grant: a grant award set aside for a specific, pre-identified grant applicant where the applicant simply completes the required administrative paper work. (No competition is required or involved.)

Nonprofit: an incorporated business where stockholders and trustees do not share in the profits. (The IRS tax-exempt 501 (c) 3 organization is created to accomplish charitable, humanitarian, or educational purposes.)

Notice of Funds Available (NOFA): a request for proposal (RFP), funding opportunity announcement (FOA), solicitation, and/or an announcement of the availability of funding.

Novice Applicant: a new applicant which has not received a discretionary grant of any type within a five-year period.

Objectives: measurable activities that will be accomplished during a grant period; used to determine whether or not a grantee is moving toward the stated goal(s).

Operating Expenses: all expenses (direct and indirect) related to the production of goods and services. (Such costs include employee wages, research, websites, utilities, consultants, bookkeeping expenses, travel, professional development, licensing, insurance, print costs, etc.)

Operating Foundation: an organization created for the sole purpose of conducting research, social welfare, or other programs as revealed by the founders and the board of directors; occasionally makes grants.

Outcome Evaluation: an evaluation/assessment/analysis that comprehensively describes an organization's programs, projects, or activities as it relates to short-term, mid-term, and long term changes (or impacts) in relation to proposed goals, objectives, and missions.

Outcome Measures: signs (indicators) that concentrate on the direct results of the proposed grant program or project.

Partnership: a formal, cooperative collaboration between two or more organizations, entities, groups, etc. that is mutually beneficial for all parties involved; involves working towards a common goal.

Pass Through: an organization that submits a proposal on behalf of a sub-grantee; takes a percentage of grant funds for administrative costs to manage the grant (e.g. submit reports, evaluations, manage funds distribution, accounting). (Sometimes, a sub-grantee is ineligible to apply for a type of grant. So, the pass through acts as the grantee in good faith so the grantee may receive funding.)

Pipeline: the process of funding applicants that scored high enough to be funded, but missed the cut off (funding threshold). (If a grantee should pass the review process and is unwilling or unable to modify their applications in order to meet the grantor's regulations and requirements and be awarded [officially], the applicant's in the pipeline are contacted and awarded those funds, as long as they agree to the terms.)

Pre-Application: the process of submitting screening information to the grantor prior to the full proposal submission; usually used in order to determine which applicants will receive an invitation to submit a full grant application. (Some Letters of Intent or Inquiry are also used as pre-applications by private funders. Although they may not be named a pre-application, the purpose and the processes are one in the same.)

Principal Investigator: primary or lead evaluator or project director.

Prison: a place where inmates are involuntarily held for committing a crime in cases where guilt is alleged and confirmed; your new home if you steal or misuse and/or embezzle state and federal funding. (Don't go to jail for money that you didn't earn. You will be caught eventually.)

Private Foundation: a nonprofit organization with directors or trustees to manage the organization, its programs and services, finances, grant awards, and processes, etc.; grant awards to programs that fall under the charitable category.

Process Evaluation: an evaluation that assesses or measures what was done, how much was done, when it was done, for whom it was done, and by whom it was done during the grant period; usually disseminated to the public and grantor.

Program Director: person responsible for overseeing a program or project. (Some Program Directors are fulltime staff overseeing day-to-day operations. Others contribute minimally to the project [such as an Executive Director]. Program Directors and Project Directors are essentially the same thing. The title of Project Director is primarily used with federal funding proposals.)

Program Income (also called Project Income): all (gross) income or revenue generated by a project; usually requested for a period. (Examples include revenues/funds generated by fundraising events, grants, interest income, donations, and fees for service.)

Program Office: the physical office where the grantor agency is located; where all activities and oversight related to a particular grant program are conducted; from where the solicitations creation, publishing, and all aspects of the application review process come; term is used by public and private funders.

Program Officers: person(s) within the Program Office responsible for the overseeing, management, and accountability of a specific (or of all) grant programs and competitions within an organization or office; often responsible for providing technical support for grantees; term used by public and private funders.

Program Regulations: the guidelines set by the program office or grant-makers used as rules and principles for operating specific grant-funded programs. (Every grant-making agency has program regulations. Some are disseminated prior to application submission; others are disseminated post award.)

Project: a formalized program or plan prepared for grant submission.

Project Period: the timeframe over which the proposed program or project will take place. (With private funders, a timeframe may or may not be set in stone [e.g. "all projects must be completed within one year of grant award"], while others may have more flexible project periods. With federal funding, timeframes are almost always set in stone and are set by legislation, program regulations, and the federal grant-making agency's funding cycle. Project periods for multi-year federal grants usually start off as one-year time periods to ensure grantees are compliant before awarding additional years.)

Proposal: an application written to a grant-maker pitching a proposed project or program for which the applicant organization is seeking funding. (Some proposals are formal. Some are templates. Some proposals are short [5-7 pages], while others are very long [40-200+ pages]. It depends on the project and the subject area. Proposals are written/prepared according to specifications and instructions provided by each funder. Every proposal you prepare will be different and modified to meet the funders' specifications. While some elements may be the same, all proposals will be different.)

Recipient: (1) the grantee. (2) the person or community benefiting from a program or service funded by a grant.

Regulations (Regs.): rules, policies, and procedures with detailed programmatic or project restrictions established by state or federal legislation; include purpose of funding, applicant qualifications that must be met in order to apply, allowable costs, any relevant criteria needed for the selection process, required or allowed activities, and other information.

Replicable: the expectation that the proposed project can be duplicated successfully with encouraging results.

Request for Proposals (RFP) (also called Request for Applications [RFA]): the formal call for proposals by the grant funder inviting applicants to apply for grant funding; Notice of Funding Ability

Review Criteria: the criteria used by independent subject matter experts, program staff, or federal staff in order to assess whether applicants have met requirements specified in an RFP for the purposes of awarding points. (The review criteria along with points assigned to each criteria is always provided in Federal grant proposals. It's not always obvious.)

Review Panel (also called Peer Review Panels or Panel Reviews): subject matter experts selected to review grant proposals because of their experience and expertise in the subject area for which the RFP was issued; read, score, and make recommendations to program staff in regards to which grant proposals/applications should be funded.

RFA: Request for Applications. Also see Request for Proposals.

RFP: See Request for Proposal

Seed Money (also called Seed funding): Funds issued to start a new project or issued to newly formed organizations as a grant or general contribution; awarded to organizations and projects that have promise.

Service Providers: individuals and agencies that provide professional services or expertise to the community.

Single Point of Contact (SPOC): the state contact that an applicant must inform when applying for federal grants. (Not all states require a single point of contact. To determine if you are required to submit a federal grant proposal to an SPOC, visit: https://www.whitehouse.gov/omb/grants_spoc/.)

Sub-Grantee (see Pass-Through for additional information): the recipient of the pass-through funds.

Supplanting: purposely reducing, ignoring, or lying about state funds (or other grant funds) in order to receive federal funds. (For example, if a state grant (or other grant) funds a line item expense in a program budget [e.g. staff member or rent] for a specific amount, you request funding for the federal government for the same expense. The agency is awarded that funding and then stashes the excess funding from the state funding. You then choose to pay for the pre-existing line item expense from newly awarded federal funding. This is a no, no, NO! Most funders discourage this behavior, but federal funders prohibit this practice. *When* caught, the agency will be forced to repay the funding and may be barred from future federal funding activities. In an age of transparency, it's in your organization's best interest to be truthful about ALL program income and revenue.)

Sustainability: an organization's or program's plan for financially and physically maintaining a program or project beyond a funding cycle or funding period.

System for Award Management (SAM) (formally known as The Central Contract Registry [CCR]): the official U.S. Government system that consolidated the capabilities of the Central Contractor Registration (CCR) /Federal Register (FedReg). (Any organization or individual wishing to do business with the government must register with SAM. It is a very long process completed online. For more information, visit: https://www.sam.gov. Beware of sites that charge to help complete the process. I'm not saying that they are not legitimate, but you need to be aware that there are no costs associated with completing the process.)

Target Area: the proposed geographical area where a service or program will operate; can be regional, county or zip code specific, or state or multi-state specified. (Whatever the target area, be sure to provide all target population data related to it. The persons within the target area represent your target population.)

Target Date: deadline.

Target Population: specific demographics towards which a program will gear services or programs. (When identifying the target population, use as much relevant and recent data available [e.g. school district data, census bureau data, Children and Family services data]. Many grant proposals fail to be funded because the applicant does not demonstrate adequate knowledge of their target population.)

Technical Assistance: assistance provided by experts or grant-makers aimed at increasing or improving an organization's capacity and/or solving program, project, or organizational problems.

Timeline: a chart comprehensively detailing programmatic or project activities for a specific timeframe; includes proposed activities, the date/timeframe on which activities will take place, the person/agency responsible for completing activities, and any milestones/indicators which will enable the grantor to verify whether the activity was completed. (For federal grants, timelines need to cover the entire funding period, even if activities are recurring and duplicative of the first year.)

Triple New Lease: a lease requiring utilities, taxes, and insurance to be paid by the tenant or occupier.

Turnkey: the duplication of a project or program whose aspects have already been created. (Sometimes organizations offer their successful grant proposal to other interested prospective applicants so they do not have to "reinvent the wheel." All the interested party needs to do is submit a fully prepared proposal with minor modifications [e.g. agency name, staff, target population/area, partners, service area].)

Unrestricted Grant (see General Operating Support for additional information): a grant that can be used for any purpose the organization needs.

White Papers: expertise articles, studies, research papers, or literature presented at conferences.

Final Thoughts

These are just a few basic definitions. They, by no means, represent all of the various terms used by grant funders. Below are some links to other nonprofit world terms. If you cannot find a term used, call the funder to ask for the definition and an example (if he/she will give you one). For novices and newbies, not understanding the terms could lead to misinterpretation of any part of a funding opportunity announcement. Misinterpretation can cause you to exclude relevant information you deemed unimportant and may cause a grant-writer to provide the wrong information within a narrative or budget. Providing incomplete and incorrect information may cause you to lose points and miss the funding threshold. Have fun learning. We all had to. I wish I had something like this when I first started. You live and you learn.

Happy hunting!

Other Online Grant Terminology Resources

School District of Osceola Florida:
http://www.osceola.k12.fl.us/depts/Grant_Management/definitions.asp

United States Department of Agriculture (USDA):
http://www.fns.usda.gov/fm/grants-terminology

Foundation Center:
http://www.foundationcenter.org/getstarted/tutorials/gfr/glossary.html

National Institutes of Health (NIH):
http://grants.nih.gov/grants/glossary.htm

National Emergency Medical Services for Children Data Analysis Resource Center (NEDARC):
http://www.nedarc.org/writingGrants/whatIsAGrant/commonGrantTerminology.html

Chaffey College:
http://www.chaffey.edu/grants/glossary.shtml

8. MAINTAINING YOUR DISCOVERED TREASURES

I'm sure you are overwhelmed by all of the information you now have at your access for grant research. Before you get too entrenched in searching and collecting goodies, I recommend creating a method to the madness. As grant-writers and researchers, we tend to collect a lot of useful, relative information over time. Some of the information we can maintain for a short time, such as information used to prepare specific grant proposals, but there are times when some of the information we run across is useful/valuable long term. I recommend maintaining several folders (hard copy and digital) in a few places. I make this recommendation for a number of reasons:

- **Staff members come and go**.
  Saving your findings to your own personal library (separate from a client's or employer's library) is just good sense. Why do all the hard work finding the grants just to lose access to the information when/if you decide to change employers? Work smarter, not harder.
- **Sharing**
  If you are a volunteer, you may be responsible for helping others find resources. If you are a staff person, you may have volunteers assisting with funds development or grant-writing. Having a central location to share information is necessary. Creating a method to share and exchange information is vital for efficiency as well as timely responsiveness.
- **Space**
  Sometimes, you may find it's simpler to print some information and save it in a folder or share it with leaders. However, it may be better to store your information in a folder on a computer or a cloud (personally, I hate clouds, but I do use them). Because none of the information collected is sensitive or confidential, clouds are appropriate. The nice thing about clouds is that you can simply invite individuals to specific folders and they are able to select the information they need. Should your computer die, or in the event you're traveling, a cloud is a great way to always maintain access to information related to grant research.
- **Crashes**
  It is not *if* a crash happens, but *when* a crash happens. A computer can crash at any time, any place, and for any reason (virus, motherboard death); there is nothing you can do about it. Having your research backed up in multiple places, as well as in hard copy, will allow you to have access to your information regardless of the situation. Be prepared. Grant-writers and researchers work really hard to find information. Don't become complacent; be ready. Be on guard. Save and back up all work.

How/Where to Store Your Information

- **Saving to Clouds**
  There are a number of resources that offer free cloud services with an email account: Microsoft Office Live, One Drive, Google Docs, Gmail, and more. Other services like Dropbox offer a certain amount of space for free (and more for all invites and new accounts you help them secure). Some of you may currently use clouds for your personal use, but I recommend creating a separate cloud to keep things clean, especially for sharing. With all of the hacking going on (OPM, Adobe, Yahoo, Gmail, Apple, etc.), nothing is safe enough to include the personal information used to set up the cloud accounts. While I recommend clouds, I do recommend safeguarding all personal information and assuming that, once you place it within the system, it is available for anyone to see (and steal). I advise using throwaway email addresses or fake information in case your account happens to be hacked.

Clouds are a great way to share work information easily. Just be mindful that they are not private.

- **Hard Copies**
  Organized hard copies are great. Of course, it's useless to buy a book on current statistics, but a library of grant funding resources could be quite useful to an individual or organization. Purchasing books, studies, and other subject matter material is a fantastic way to diversify the way you conduct research. The only downside of hard copy libraries is that people tend to "borrow" and never return the materials to their rightful homes. If using this method, you will likely need to develop some type of check-out system or other way to keep track of the hard copies. If you are not able to do so, then by all means go digital with clouds. You can also print material from your online research endeavors that may be reused at a later date. Hard copies are also a fantastic way to give the eyes a break from hours upon hours of viewing computer screens.

- **Flash Drives**
  Hate storing things on your computers and clouds? Flash drives are a great way to store your digital research material. They are inexpensive, can hold many gigabytes of data, make sharing digital materials easier, and can be carried anywhere, anytime, and any place.

- **Favorites Toolbar**
  Don't be afraid to save useful information to your favorites tool bar, especially items you may need to access frequently, like databases.

Types of Information To Save

- Data/Statistics
- Any funder guidelines
- Current or old funding opportunity announcements, solicitations, and requests for proposals
- Compiled web addresses of private funder websites
- Subject Matter Studies
- Old grant proposals found online (winners and losers)
- Sample job descriptions
- Any laws and regulations tied to your specific funding needs
- Any state legislation
- Contact information for state and federal representatives/elected officials
- Current and past collaboration agreements (memorandums)
- Letters of Support
- Relative news articles
- Old Memorandums and Letters of Agreement
- Slide presentations
- Surveys, needs assessments, evaluations, and confidentiality agreements used to secure surveys (if/when applicable)

Final Thoughts

There are many things to save and there are so many ways to manage how those items are stored.

Developing a system early on prevents items from being placed in any random location where they may or may not be rediscovered at a later date. There are some items you will use throughout your grant research and grant-writing career. Learning how to manage the information that you will need and share is quite important as it helps with efficiency, which is extremely important with grant-writing and research projects—especially when working on short deadlines.

9. RESEARCH ASSISTANCE: DEVELOPING RESEARCH TEAMS

Grant proposal development and grant funding research are huge, laborious tasks. Depending on the type of grant proposal you are preparing (private or public), the required research may be very extensive, taking weeks to complete. Personal working preferences, time constraints, number of experienced or interested staff, as well as the availability of unrestricted revenues to hire or outsource such a position are all factors in whether an organization hires/uses a team for any and all proposal development efforts. Because the research portion is the most important aspect of grant proposal development, it is important to assemble the right team members in order to ensure you gather the best nuggets for describing your needs to find the best grant funding resources.

Ideal Characteristics of Potential Research Team Members

The types of grant proposals you are writing and developing (e.g. state, federal, private, small, large) will determine the types of individuals you will need on your team, if there is a team component at all. Unless you have a keen understanding of the entire process (writing, reviewing, and awarding), I do not recommend attempting to prepare federal proposals alone. The team approach is wise when preparing larger proposals, as it allows individuals on the research team to comprehensively research and prepare one specific section of the grant funding criteria. In order to gain a competitive edge and have a greater chance at scoring high enough to be awarded a grant, your application must demonstrate adequate research. When selecting research team members, be sure to select persons who demonstrate specific qualities:

- **Passionate and knowledgeable about the nonprofit/public sectors**
  If a person is unaware of how the sector works, how funding is secured, or the expectations of funders, it will be really difficult to convince them of the importance of finding the correct information to support the applicant organization's need(s).

- **Book-loving**
  Researchers must *love* consuming information (reading), comprehending the information, and describing (verbally) what they have read in a convincing manner. These individuals must know how to find information. Whether it be from periodicals, extensive institutional research databases, government gateways, the library, etc., these individuals need to be comfortable with reading and researching.

- **Detail-oriented**
  Research team members must be able to comprehend and adhere to solicitation or funding opportunity deadlines. They must also be able to meet the research team's timelines. If you cannot get the information you need in a timely fashion, then the team is useless. Being able to understand and follow instructions are key to ensuring you will hit all targets on time.

- **Pleasant to work with**
  No one wants an adversarial person on his/her team. A person that's constantly bucking against everyone, a consistent complainer, an under-handed sneaky Pete that is always asking questions, wanting to do things their own way, gossiping and/or creating havoc and discord among team members and leaders is a problem that must be dealt with before it begins (don't hire him/her). Nothing is worse than walking into a team meeting knowing one of team members is possessed by some spirit of trouble at every turn. Pick your team members wisely, as that one problem

person can make or break your proposal endeavor efforts. They may also put such a bad taste in the mouths of good team members that they dislike the process and lose all desire to assist the organization in finding and securing grant funds. If you are this person and you are reading this book, *please stop.* If you're not sure, then ask. The same applies for team leaders. If you're confrontational, extremely critical, hard to talk to, hard to get along with, ignorant, and/or outwardly disrespectful to team members, you (too) are ruining the process for all parties involved. Step back and take a look at the situation. Are you helping the process or hurting it? Not sure, then ask. Anonymously of course, but (by all means) ask.

- **Able to put personal biases aside**
  When searching for data related to need, there is no time for personal biases. You may need to call and ask local organizations for information. Instead of thinking of them as "friends," you and your associates may not have a working relationship with these entities (maybe because, your organizations are similar, you may not enter into their territory). Perhaps they got funding that you thought your organization should have received. Whatever the issue is, put it to bed. If there is a needs assessment or other information that could help support your cause, lay the personal biases aside to get what you need. Your goal is to get funded, not walk around believing another organization is your enemy. The field is wide, and the ranges of funding sources available are vast. Be the bigger person and do your job well. High-quality research validates need. Being objective is a *must* in this process.

- **Dedicated to the mission/cause**
  If a person isn't dedicated or vested in the cause, they are not likely to be a great research partner. Whether it's a paid colleague or a volunteer, we all know people who are with an organization for motives other than the cause or mission (e.g. public service obligations or pay check). These individuals may have been assigned to the research project by organizational leadership, so you're stuck like chuck with them. When there is a choice in the matter, be certain to select individuals that care about the mission and the organization seeking funding. It makes life so much easier. These people don't need to be perfect, but they most certainly need to care. In the event you are stuck with the former individuals, try to help them understand how they are personally connected to the mission or cause. Helping them understand why it should be important to them may help them become more engaged and change their perspective.

I could go on to name a few other characteristics, but they would be just some personal pet peeves. We all have things that work and don't work for us when working on a team. You will need to determine your own deal breakers, then figure out how to select and work with the individuals that will form your team.

Outsourcing Research

Outsourcing some aspects of grant proposal development is becoming big business these days. Most people hate to conduct the research. I enjoy this task. There are also some organizations that simply don't have the capacity to complete all aspects of the proposal development process. They may have more money than time. Some may have more volunteers or staff than money. Whatever your preference, understanding that there is no "one size fits all" method for this process is key. You must do what works best for your proposal development efforts within your individual time and financial constraints. Should you decide not to keep the research aspects of the process in-house, allow me to provide some hints that may helpful to as you make your choice:

- **Weigh your individual or organizational finances first.** Outsourcing to the right person will cost you something. Sadly, outsourcing to the wrong person will cost you something as well. Negotiating rates upfront and understanding what you'll be getting for your money is vital. Understanding the time and resources required to conduct such searches is also important; you will understand why a consultant is charging what they quote.

- **Understand how complex research can be.** Grant funding research and grant proposal development research can be quite complex. It is important to communicate your expectations, needs, desires, and the timeframe in which the work will need to be completed to the person hired to conduct research on your behalf.

- **Understand that consultants are different.** There is no one way to conduct research. Individual consultants have different methods for conducting research along with different resources they use to find what is needed on behalf of their clients. While being a part of the process is vital, allowing the consultant to work in their element is key. Not doing so compromises the process and your organization will suffer because of it.

- **Consultants come in all varieties and from all backgrounds.** Do not infer that if you pay a well-established, more expensive researcher or company that you will get the highest quality of work. Also, do not assume that a new or lower priced consultant means lower quality work. Ask for references, go with your instinct, and do not allow money alone to dictate your decisions in regards to selecting a consultant to which to outsource.

- **Volunteers and interns can be a saving grace.** For organizations with little or no unrestricted funding, hiring consultants or outsourcing certain aspects of the proposal process is out of the question. Connecting with your volunteers or colleges and universities in order to get the job done is an awesome way to build a resource library and get the information needed to apply and secure grant resources. If you have volunteers or plan to develop a volunteer recruitment process, be sure to inventory the assets of your volunteers. Find out the answers to the following questions:

    - What skills do they have?
    - What are their educational backgrounds?
    - How much time will they have to dedicate to the project?
    - Have they exhibited a skill or interest in grant proposal development?

Now, I'm not advocating turning volunteers into slaves on behalf of the organization. Please do not abuse and take advantage of the kindness of your local volunteer pool. Volunteers talk and, once they spread the word that you run a horrible workplace that takes advantage of your high-quality, lively volunteer pool, you can kiss them goodbye; they won't be coming back. I am advocating utilizing resources easily accessible to your organization for the short-term benefit of the organization. Sometimes, an organization's volunteers are great assets and they are able to stop the bleeding short and mid-term. The long-term solution, however, is always to find ways to invest in a person or team which is more sustainable. Be progressive. Be forward thinking. Find ways to sustain the most vital role of an organization. Without funds, you absolutely cannot operate efficiently. Consider volunteers for your research and funds development efforts when unrestricted funds are low or non-existent. Advertise on Craigslist (yes, it's great for free recruitment) or search places such as the United Way, college and university nonprofit programs, English departments, high schools, and senior centers.

Shopping Locally for Researchers

One thing I hear constantly (and I experience personally) is that agencies and organizations tend to hire outside of their area instead of using local talent. Sometimes, people are unaware of resources that exist in their local communities. I love working locally because I'm able to visit my worksites, meet with clients, see their work, and better understand what's going on in my community. Unfortunately, my clients are almost always from outside of my state. For whatever reason, consultants don't do a great job of connecting and networking locally, and those in need of such services rarely, if ever, connect with the proper resources to secure grant funding. Before leaving your community to find researchers for your grant-writing project, attempt to shop locally first. Keeping dollars in your local community is important now more than ever. Ask other nonprofits, Chambers of Commerce, and nonprofit associations. Search online for grant-writers. Sometimes, grant-writers can provide an array of services; they simply state that they are grant-writers, assuming clients will understand they know how to do everything entailed in the proposal development process. When in doubt, ask.

Outsourcing to Colleagues in Collaboratives

When working in collaborative settings, you will find that proposal development, planning, meeting, and strict timelines are essential. Different agencies, different partners, and/or different individuals involved in the proposal development process almost always have other jobs to do besides the planning, research, and development of grant proposals. Being respectful of everyone's time is key to a healthy, successful relationship during and after the proposal development process. Here are a few tips for successful group research and proposal development collaboratives:

- **Write it down.** For those with social work and human service backgrounds, you know that, if you did not write your information down, then there's no evidence that you did it. At the onset, make sure each partner is fully aware of their specific role, their specific area of research, and targets/deadlines for information submission. Usually, there is one person responsible for compiling all the information. This person should be responsible for taking notes and disseminating the details to everyone in a timely, orderly fashion. Be sure to send all correspondence electronically and include all team members so that no one is able to shirk their responsibilities.

- **Provide handouts.** At each meeting, be sure everyone signs in and everyone receives handouts (e.g. meeting minutes, timetables, proposal updates, progress reports, responsibility chart). The more information, the better. Make it plain for all to see and understand.

- **Keep everyone honest.** If you are a team leader, be sure to keep everyone honest. Hold their feet to the fire. Create a team proposal development process by identifying everybody's responsibility. Make it an inclusive, team-building activity. Also, be available for team members to answer questions and address any concerns. Be professional and swift in delegating responsibilities to team members in the event that someone falls down on the job. Proposals are time-sensitive, so act accordingly.

- **Explain and answer questions. Then, explain some more.** A person on the team must be able to handily comprehend and explicitly explain the criteria. In order for team members to understand what they must look for when conducting research (as well as to provide it), they must know specifically what the grant funder wants to know via the criteria in the funding opportunity announcement. Explain the information in the application that's relative to each perspective team member, allowing them to ask questions. Provide an abundance of examples and guidance regarding what information is needed to satisfy the criteria. Provide some leads on where to search (locally and online). Ensure all team members are comfortable with their component of the research project and allow a Q & A session for clarification. Make sure team members take notes as well and help them own their contributions.

- **Make sure you have enough time to complete the research.** Application deadlines are non-negotiable. Because the team leader or applicant organization can control no one's actions except his/her own, you must convene quickly in order to get the project started. You must also be willing to decline to start a project if a project cannot be prepared in a reasonable timeframe without placing excessive, unnecessary stress or pressure on team players. When in doubt, take a tally. Never go at it alone. The results you get may not be the results you want.

Final Thoughts

I have heard many horror stories of teams that fell apart before some collaborative research projects were complete because one or two team members decided not to complete their components of the research project. They dropped the ball and other members had to pick up those balls, dragging them to the finish line. Some teams are able to recover and get the job done by any means necessary. Others are completely caught off guard and are unable to recoup the time lost. They were forced to abandon the grant application and wait another three or five years until the next grant cycle returns (for federal grants). It's heart breaking, it's stressful, and it's certainly a shame. Select team members wisely and work on reasonable timelines. Work smarter, not harder.

When outsourcing research, there is a lot of trust involved. At some point, you lose control of an aspect of the proposal development process. You must trust the person or group you turned the research aspect of the project over to. Remember that communication is key when delegating must happen. Never assume your team understands or knows what you already know. Never assume you already know everything (you do not). And remember, *no one* is perfect (including you). Leave ample time to review, edit, correct, cite, and revise any research contributed to the proposal. Everyone will be happier and more fruitful if you do.

10. CLOSING

My hope is that you have gained ample knowledge about where and how to search for grant funding. The purpose of this book is to provide opportunities to ALL grant-seeking agencies and groups, not just to the big organizations with the most money, not just to the organizations with the longest track record, and not just to the organizations and agencies that have the ability to hire development staffers and experienced consultants. I desire every size of organization at the grassroots level to have the same opportunities, evening the playing field when it comes to knowledge of resources. There are many great resources on writing grants (online classes, books, college certifications, trainings), but not many resources on the actual techniques related to grant research. It's quite different from grant-writing and a totally different mindset is needed in order to simply *begin* the process. I hope the information provided supplied a method to this madness we call grant-writing. You can't write a grant if you don't know where to find a grant. And if you find a grant that you are able to apply for, you can't possibly be successful if you have no idea how to compile the information in order to tell a great story—a story which demonstrates need.

Readers may need to break this book apart and work on certain sections that are of particular interest to them first. Each and every section is significant and relevant. There is neither waste nor excess here. You have the meat and potatoes—no frills, no fluff, only the real deal. I wished I had this when I first started writing grants. Instructors taught me well on how to develop and write strong proposals. What I wasn't taught was the research piece of proposal development. It took me years (literally) to understand how grant research and storytelling actually works. Even then, it took years of conducting federal grant reviews to put the entire picture together. If you are just coming into the world of grant proposal development and grant-writing, welcome. Do not think it will be easy, because it will not. Do not think people will freely offer resources and all the knowledge they have secured over the years either through formal education, trial and error, or working in the field. They will not and you should not expect them to. Each and every one of us had to learn this skill/craft while honing our skills on the fly. I have said this throughout the book, but please let me reiterate it. Practice makes perfect. No one will be able to "get this" without sacrificing time and energy. When I first started as a grant-writer, I felt like I was on an island all alone. I lived in a really small rural town. There were not many people doing what I wanted to do. If they knew how, they certainly weren't sharing. I had to learn on my own.

This field can be a bit cold sometimes and we grant-writers can be cut throat (yes, we work in the public sector, but we can be territorial just like the competition between Walgreens and CVS). Grant-writing is a technical skill that not everyone can easily do. Many of us have acquired this technical skill via the school of hard knocks (on the job training). Some of us have had the skill "forced" upon us by our employers, while others seek it out on their own via continuing educational opportunities. Finding answers to questions related to grant-writing and research can sometimes feel like you're in the wild, wild, west. We are often a very unregulated sector in many ways, and the sector is not always "conformed," which can make learning difficult. With this understanding, if you ask and don't get the answers you need, keep asking. There are many online forums and professional associations you can join. I gained the greatest wealth of knowledge from the Professional Grant-writers Group on LinkedIn[1]. It is a private group where members can pose questions about grant-writing and all things related to funding in the nonprofit sector and hold vibrant discussions about trends, writing tips, etc. There are a number of people who are there to simply toot their own horns and self-promote, but if you filter through all of that to find relevant threads and watch out for posters with comments related to your

---

[1] https://www.linkedin.com/groups?gid=3680430

needs, you should be able to learn quite a bit. You will find that some people never offer up anything of value and you will find a number of people that love to help as much as possible. Sometimes we get the same questions over and over and we don't always answer them. Before posing questions, be sure to search to ensure that the question hasn't already been answered. Also, please understand, as I have stated earlier, there some things that experienced writers and consultants just are not going to share with you, no matter how you pose the questions. Roll up your sleeves and do the work. Let it become a labor of love.

Grant research must become an intricate part of your grant proposal development process or you will *NEVER* become successful at it. I love to tell my classes that, when it comes to grant proposals, if you don't clearly illustrate the need, you do not need any grant funding. A clear illustration of a need is a call to action for funders. Make them *want* to write your organization/project a check. Your research will determine the comprehensiveness of your need statement or narrative. The better you get at researching and providing compelling evidence, the more success you'll have at winning grants. Great research also enables writers to develop strong approaches to solve the problems for which they are seeking funding. While describing the need is likely the single most important aspect of proposal development, the second most important aspect of proposal development will be the approach used to address the need you bring forward. Being informed is the best way for you to kill these two birds. It really isn't difficult once you learn the ropes. In the beginning though, it will be very painful and time-consuming. Unless you are a bookworm and love reading any and all things, the beginning will have you bored out of your mind. I strongly recommend you research information related to people, children, agriculture, business, and social issues within your own local community. Search by zip code(s), age group(s), race/ethnicity, or any socio-economic indicator tracked. What you discover will (hopefully) catch your eye and inspire you to continue your research.

My final piece of advice is don't give up. In the beginning, if you are just starting the entire proposal development process, your applications will be ugly and you may not be successful, especially if you are not a strong writer or storyteller. Don't be discouraged. I had a lot of fake friends and old colleagues that told me I couldn't do it. Sometimes, you will be lightyears ahead of the people around you and extremely misunderstood. Don't give up—keep plugging away until you start seeing the fruits of your labor. Once you begin your research, you will learn so many things related to how our society works as well as how funding flows from Washington, D.C. into cities and towns across America. You will eventually begin to speak differently, listen differently, and see the world in which you live differently. It won't be a bad thing or a good thing; it will be something that eventually just *happens*. You will never run out of topics to discuss in social gatherings. You will be coveted by lots of organizations and individuals who would simply love to pick your brain and have you help them with a project they are working on. I call it a form of pimping. You do all the work, all the learning, all the writing, all the advising, and all the finding of resources—they reap all the benefits for free. You will have to learn how to handle your newly found fame. Share your skillset wisely or run the risk of being overrun with request for your skillset.

I wish you the best in your grant research endeavor and I would really like to hear from you in regards to your thoughts about the book. Please leave an honest review if you purchased this book online. You can email me via my website simplegrantresearch.info or simply visit my "Contact Us" page to leave a comment or recommendation for the next edition. I'll be adding additional information as I continue to compile and categorize my resources to expand the content. My goal for this research guide is to be the "go to" book for grant-writers and researchers. I want to provide the most helpful content for organizations and individuals, whether they are on a reservation in the deserts of California, on the Southside of Chicago, in Guam, in a church in McCormick, South Carolina, or in the

Appalachian Mountains. No matter where you are in America, no matter what your level of experience, this book can provide some support and assistance to you without breaking the bank. I realize that many organizations are unable to pay for expensive professional development trainings or travel to offsite grant-writing workshops. My hope is that this book is all you will ever need to get your grant research tasks completed.

Good luck. I want to thank you so much for purchasing this book. I hope you love reading it as much as I loved writing it. It is a dream come true. Look for future material from my series "yet to be titled." I am looking forward to creating more useful content and materials and providing access to the masses—no frills, no strings, just information. I strive to provide grant-writers and proposal developers content that I wish I had. Again, best wishes in your endeavors and don't forget to recommend this book if you enjoyed it.

NK

ABOUT THE AUTHOR

Nikki Kirk, B.S.
Author, Grant-Writer, Consultant, Trainer

Nikki Kirk has over 10 years of experience in management, grant-writing, nonprofit program development, community economic development, and nonprofit management consulting. She achieved a 5-year career with Kirk's Consulting Services, where she acts as the founder and CEO and serves customers in a number of capacities including capacity-building, nonprofit compliance, Pre-K-12 education program development, nonprofit incorporation, strategic planning, evaluations, mergers, dissolutions, and other areas revolving around the nonprofit lifecycle. She has extensive experience in strategic initiatives and operational responsibilities grounded in information technology and performance management. She specializes in working with small, underserved, and underrepresented nonprofit groups and organizations.

Nikki continues an active role with both private and public companies globally. She has worked in the capacities as nonprofit incorporator, advisor, and board member for early-stage and middle-stage not-for-profit entities and has provided a wide range of nonprofit offerings including eLearning, compliance and corporate governance, resource development, employee sourcing and recruiting, grant readiness, capacity building, and federal, state, private, and foundation grant-writing and reviews.

During her business career in South Carolina, Nikki was involved with a number of civic and charitable organizations. She served on the Greenwood County First Steps board, Community of Dreams, Square board, Crossroads Pregnancy Center, and Boy Scouts of America board and she held various leadership roles at the Sexual Assault and Children's Advocacy Center of Northeast Georgia, Upper Savannah Care HIV/AIDS Consortium, Greenwood Chamber of Commerce, Grace Community Church, Piedmont Technical College, Calhoun Falls Charter School, and on the Greenwood County School District 50 Advisory Board and the Emerald High School Improvement Council.

Nikki holds a B.S. in Business Administration from Franklin University in Columbus, Ohio and has a certification in grant-writing as well as grant evaluations from Research Associates via the University of South Carolina in Columbia, South Carolina. She currently teaches grant-writing to law enforcement and public safety organizations, nonprofits, and faith communities. She also is a national grant-writing trainer for Grant Central USA, located in Sacramento, California.

Made in the USA
Middletown, DE
14 October 2018